History's Great
STRUCTURES

The Great Wall
of China

Other titles in the *History's Great Structures* series include:

The Eiffel Tower

The Medieval Castle

The Parthenon of Ancient Greece

The Roman Colosseum

Shakespeare's Globe Theater

The World Trade Center

History's Great STRUCTURES

The Great Wall of China

Cindy Jenson-Elliott

ReferencePoint Press®

San Diego, CA

© 2014 ReferencePoint Press, Inc.
Printed in the United States

For more information, contact:
ReferencePoint Press, Inc.
PO Box 27779
San Diego, CA 92198
www.ReferencePointPress.com

LIBRARY OF CONGRESS CATALOGING-IN-PUBLICATION DATA

Jenson-Elliott, Cynthia L.
 The Great Wall of China : part of the history's great structures series / by Cindy Jenson-Elliott.
   pages cm. -- (History's great structures series)
 Includes bibliographical references and index.
 ISBN-13: 978-1-60152-534-5 (hardback)
 ISBN-10: 1-60152-534-6 (hardback)
 1. Great Wall of China (China) I. Title.
 DS793.G67J46 2014
 931--dc23
                                                        2013010772

CONTENTS

IMPORTANT EVENTS IN THE HISTORY OF THE GREAT WALL OF CHINA

CA. 2300 BC

Trade routes begin to open up between China and the West.

CA. 221 BC

The Qin Dynasty, under which many walls are joined to form one great wall, begins.

CA. 2700 BC

The Han cradle area develops in China.

CA. 5000 BC

The first walls are built around Chinese agricultural villages.

CA. 475 BC

The Warring States period begins.

5000 BC	3500	2000	500

CA. 2500 BC

The Chinese begin to control water use through hydraulic projects; land productivity increases, agriculture advances, and the first gradations in wealth appear in China.

CA. 1500 BC

Changing climate pushes people north to Mongolia, where a nomadic, pastoralist culture develops.

CA. 206 BC

The Han Dynasty, which expands wall building, begins.

220 AD

The Three Kingdoms period begins with three powerful dynasties—Wei, Wu, and Shu. Each kingdom creates its own wall systems.

2008

China hosts its first-ever Olympic Games; the Great Wall is used as a prominent symbol of the country's cultural and economic achievements.

1368

The Ming Dynasty, considered the greatest of China's wall-building dynasties, begins.

1972

US president Richard Nixon makes a historic visit to China; he tours some of the country's cultural and artistic treasures, including the Great Wall.

681

The Tang Dynasty begins, bringing China a time of peace and prosperity.

500 AD   1000   1500   2000

1912

The Republic of China is founded.

1949

The People's Republic of China is founded; the Great Wall is touted as a symbol of China's greatness.

CA. 1200

Genghis Khan begins Mongol military campaigns across Eurasia; he and his successors go on to rule China and much of the known world.

386

The Northern and Southern Dynasties period begins, which is a time of cultural mixing and immigration among the peoples who live near the wall.

Great Wall, Great People

The Great Wall traces the sharp ridges of China's mountains like spines on the back of a sleeping dragon. As broad as a road and as tall as a mountain in places, the Great Wall is a symbol of China's unity as a nation and its separateness as a civilization. It is a symbol of China's push to claim the future and of its links to the past.

The Great Wall represents China's image of itself—as a powerful dragon waking and then stretching from the past to the future as a single, great people. The wall is immense and beautiful to see.

The Long Wall

In the Mandarin Chinese language, the Great Wall is called *changcheng*, translated as "long wall" or "city wall." The Great Wall is not actually a single wall stretching across the entire northern border of China. It is many walls built over millennia, joined together in places and broken by gaps in others. It is a loose configuration of great and less-than-great walls built by emperors and dynasties using a multitude of building methods and technologies over twenty-four hundred years. Some segments of these walls are majestic, intact, and well maintained, but others have been worn by wind and water, eroded to a mere line in the blowing sand—a dusty memory.

Author and Asia expert Claire Roberts writes that China's

walls possess the scale and serpentine majesty of no other heritage structure. No matter whether they are regarded as part of an early and impressive system of integrated military defence, a symbol of containment and oppression or a human folly of extraordinary proportions, the Great Wall of China is a grand idea that has imprinted itself on the minds of people throughout the world.[1]

Unlike many of humanity's great ancient structures, the Great Wall was made with materials that came from the place where it was erected. In areas with only sand and soil, the wall is built primarily from dirt tamped down inside a wall-shaped frame. In areas where the wall traverses mountains of stone, the wall is made from rocks. Some historians say that this is why the wall, immense as it is, is not visible from space. It blends perfectly into the landscape, created from it and camouflaged by it.

Scientists and historians have long argued about the length of the Great Wall. Because it has only recently been accurately surveyed and measured, reports on its length have differed dramatically. Even different articles in the same Chinese newspaper carry different claims—from 3,900 miles (6,276 km) to 30,000 miles (42,280 km) long. Recent research conducted by the China Great Wall Society in conjunction with the Chinese government suggests that the wall is more than 13,000 miles (20,921 km) long and stretches across fifteen provinces. Much of the disagreement over the wall's length depends on which sections one considers to be part of the Great Wall. The problem is, however, that historians differ on this point.

Some historians believe that any northern fortification could be considered part of the Great Wall. Others believe that for a wall to qualify as part of the Great Wall, it must have been built by ethnic Chinese people, not by people of the north who ruled China at different times throughout history. Others believe that to qualify as part of the Great Wall, a segment of wall must be at least 62 miles (100 km) long.

Some early Chinese records claim the Great Wall is *wanli* long— ten thousand *li* long, with a *li* being an ancient measurement of about 0.3 miles (0.5 km). However, *ten thousand* was also historically a term

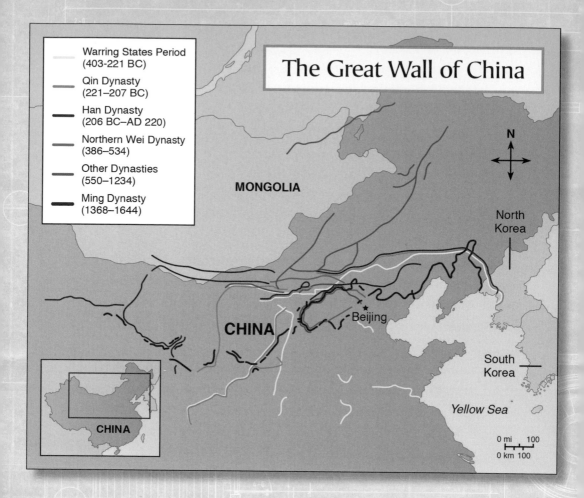

The Great Wall of China

Warring States Period (403-221 BC)
Qin Dynasty (221–207 BC)
Han Dynasty (206 BC–AD 220)
Northern Wei Dynasty (386–534)
Other Dynasties (550–1234)
Ming Dynasty (1368–1644)

MONGOLIA

N

North Korea

CHINA

Beijing

South Korea

Yellow Sea

CHINA

0 mi   100
0 km 100

of exaggeration, like saying that the moon is a *gazillion* miles away. So a *wanli* wall was just a very, very long wall.

A Meandering, Fragmented Path

Cheng Dalin, a historian who is also the photographer and author of *The Great Wall of China*, spent much of his professional life exploring the Great Wall. Over the course of five years, some accounts say he covered and photographed over 18,000 miles (28,968 km) of the wall. Even he, however, claims to have seen only 85 percent of the wall.

Walking the Great Wall today, intrepid travelers would have to cross deserts, brave precipitous mountain peaks, traverse ridges, and ford rivers to follow the wall's tumbling, crumbling path from the Gobi Desert to the Yellow Sea. Even then, they would miss portions of the wall. This is because the Great Wall does not always follow a straight path. In some areas the wall meanders into dead ends, sends spurs across valleys, and splits into fragments around ridges.

Originally built to defend China against its enemies to the north, the Great Wall has never been a perfect, impenetrable border. It has persisted, however, as a psychological barrier, a line marking the difference and distance between "civilized" Chinese societies and "barbarian" outsiders. Today the Great Wall of China continues to play an important role in China's vision of itself as an exceptional people with a long, proud history and culture.

But the Great Wall of China represents much more than a symbol of one nation. As historian Cheng states, it is "among the world's most impressive architectural achievements, not just as a Chinese cultural treasure but also as part of a shared or global cultural heritage."[2]

CHAPTER ONE

Before the Great Wall

During the middle Stone Age, or Mesolithic period—long before the first rocks were put into place on what came to be known as the Great Wall—China was home to seminomadic hunting, gathering, and fishing cultures. They moved with the seasons and used the plains to hunt and the vast rivers of the south for food. They gathered the seeds of wild grasses and other plants, roving the high plains and low valleys.

Archaeologists have found evidence of human habitation in central China dating back to the fifth millennium BC. Scientists have uncovered decorated pottery, polished jade carvings, animal bones, and tortoiseshell decorations. These artifacts are evidence of a people who practiced farming and handicrafts and most likely worshipped their ancestors in complex ceremonies.

Scientists conjecture that, over time, some cultures in China began to practice swidden, or shifting, agriculture. In shifting agricultural practices, a family or community cleared land of trees and other native plants and planted crops. When the soil lost its productivity, the group shifted to a new area, letting the first lie fallow. Unlike settled agriculture, swidden agriculture yielded relatively poor results for the amount of labor required.

Archaeological evidence suggests that by at least 2700 BC, during the Neolithic, or new Stone Age, period, human beings in China began to settle into permanent agricultural villages at the junctures of the Wei and Yellow Rivers. The region had a temperate climate and a long, warm growing season. The meandering, changing courses of rivers and streams over millennia had created deep, rich deposits of fertile soil. From this starting point, settled agriculture spread throughout the region, bounded to the south by the Yangtze River, into an area that has been called the Han cradle of Chinese civilization.

A Hydraulic Civilization

The rich soil, abundant rivers, and broad valleys of this region were well suited to agriculture. The highly variable rainfall was not. In some years it rained so much the rivers overflowed their banks and flooded fields. In other years it did not rain enough. If people were to use the region for permanent agricultural communities, they would

This archaeological site in China, dating to the Neolithic period, has yielded human skeletons and implements of stone and bone. Artifacts like these help support ideas about the beginnings of permanent settlements in China.

RAMMED-EARTH METHOD FOR BUILDING WALLS

In building and connecting sections of the first walls, the Shang Dynasty used a method that would continue to be used throughout Chinese history: rammed earth. Rammed-earth walls were constructed by building a wooden frame or box, placing dry dirt inside it, and then ramming the dirt into place with wooden poles attached to stone, bronze, or, later, iron clubs. Rammed-earth walls were built one layer at a time, with the frame and walls rising to successively higher levels.

At the bottom of a rammed-earth wall, builders often created a base of stone rubble. Between each layer of earth, they also added pieces of bamboo as a binder to speed the drying process and strengthen the wall in much the same way that hay or grass was mixed into mud in the American Southwest to create adobe. Rammed-earth walls were so hard that some have survived to the present day. But they were not as hard as stone, brick, and mortar, and they often were eroded by wind and water.

Rammed earth is used today by construction companies interested in natural building methods. Rather than ramming earth by hand, however, today giant compression machines similar to jackhammers are used to compact earth into place inside frames.

need to control the water. They would need to be able to move water closer to arable lands and divert water away from fields when there was too much.

Controlling the flow of water was—and remains today—no small feat. The labor required to dig channels to divert and manipulate the natural flow of water was too much for one farmer or family to handle. Farmers needed help from many hands. So people began to come together into farming villages to do what they could not do on their own: create systems to irrigate their fields. Progress in Chinese agriculture required people to live and work together on these first public works projects.

Some historians believe that Chinese civilization has been primarily shaped by its need and ability to manipulate water through communal labor. Historian Owen Lattimore calls China a "hydraulic civilization" because the growth of Chinese society went hand in hand with the development of water projects. He points out that "the control of soil and water in combination lay only within the reach of groups of people helping each other to dig larger channels and perhaps to build embankments that would keep flood water out of bottom lands."[3] The ability to muster labor and technology for large-scale projects—whether for walls or water control—would be important to China throughout history.

An Expanding Population

By 2500 BC, land productivity—the quantity of crops produced per acre—was increasing. Not only was the landscape fertile and the soil easy to work, the region provided water, stone, and timber for building and fuel. Irrigation could be controlled through canals and diversions, providing a steady source of water for agriculture. As agriculture shifted from swidden to permanent, irrigated farming, the population grew.

Around 2500 BC, scientists believe, the Han cradle area supported hundreds if not thousands of farming communities. With increased farming productivity, it was now possible to produce more grain than a community needed to survive—a surplus. Communities began storing surplus grain. Scientists contend that, with these surpluses, Chinese society developed its first gradations in wealth and status—those who were rich and powerful, and those who were poor and landless.

The Han cradle area also had another advantage that increased these gradations in wealth. It was close to developing trade routes that extended from central Asia to what is now Iraq and the Arabian Peninsula and oases beyond. Trade was essential to the expansion of Chinese agricultural civilization. Evidence of trade can be found at archaeological sites throughout the cradle area, according to historian Jonathan Fryer. "Primitive tools and ornaments have been dug up in places throughout China, as well as some magnificent painted pottery whose swirling designs in red, black, and white show a resemblance to those discovered in southern Russia, suggesting some sort of cultural link between China and central Asia around 2000 B.C."[4]

The cradle area lay at the juncture of several trans-Asian trade routes, creating a confluence of cultural influences that were integrated into the early Han agricultural civilization. Early traders brought domesticated animals, such as sheep and cattle, and grain crops, such as millet and wheat, from what is now Iraq in the Middle East to Chinese villages. Later, contact with cultures from the southwest brought the domestication of water buffaloes and, most importantly, terraced agriculture for rice production. These products and practices increased food production and nutrition in the area, which further added to Han population and cultural expansion.

Shaping the Land

The success and expansion of Han agriculture had the effect of expanding Han society. More crops meant better nutrition. And better nutrition led to a larger population. The more people there were, the more land was needed to feed and support the growing population.

Population pressures forced some cultures, as well as new generations of farmers, to migrate to new areas. Some areas were well suited to agriculture. Other land was less suited to farming. Farmers began to develop skills for farming steeper slopes and dryer plains.

On hillsides surrounding alluvial plains and deltas, farmers began to shape, trim, and terrace the landscape. Mountains of loess, a yellow, compacted, highly erosive, wind-blown soil, were cut and flattened. Farmers created terraces that could be farmed without causing erosion. Rolling hills became terraced farms, carved and sculpted by the new civilizations rising up from the plains.

As population pressures increased in the Han region, and the land became more and more subdivided within villages and families, migration became essential. More aggressive groups pushed less powerful neighbors out of prime agricultural areas, forcing them farther and farther north onto land that became drier and less hospitable to agriculture. These groups tried farming the higher,

During the Han cradle period, new agricultural practices led to more crops and better nutrition. Farmers of the period began experimenting with terracing (similar to the view in this photograph), which enabled them to grow crops on hillsides.

steeper, drier land in these areas, which came to be known as the steppes of Mongolia.

The people of this region practiced a mixture of scratch, or subsistence, farming and animal husbandry. In dry areas of the northwest, in what is now Gansu and Xinjiang, the people settled into communities but cared for animals around oases of water. In the northeast, near what is now Manchuria, people practiced agriculture near rivers and hunted and fished where the land was drier. And in the Ordos region, a northward loop of the Yellow River south of what is now Mongolia, the climate made the area suitable for a mixture of animal herding and agriculture.

A Changing Climate and a New Culture

As populations migrated and changed their home territories, the climate was also changing. By 1500 BC, rainfall became so scarce in the steppes of Mongolia, north of the Ordos, that agriculture became impossible. The people living in these northern areas began to change their ways to adapt to the new requirements of the dry land. They developed practices better adapted to their new home. A new way of life and a new culture began to emerge on the high steppes—a culture based around domesticated animals as a primary resource rather than farmed crops. This new way of life was called pastoralism.

Unlike the Han farmers, pastoralists were mobile rather than sedentary. They did not cultivate the land but instead let it remain as grasslands and allowed their domestic animals—horses and sheep—to graze. They followed their herds to seasonal grazing lands, up into high altitudes in the summer and lower areas in winter. Their homes were temporary and movable tent-like structures made from the skins of animals.

They depended on their animals for all their needs. They ate their meat and milk products. They made clothing from animal skins and wool. They traveled and hunted on horses, firing arrows from springy bows while riding full speed across the plains. It was a culture perfectly and sustainably suited to the dry steppes.

In the Ordos region, at the margins of agrarian and pastoral cultures, culture clash became inevitable. On the one hand were the agriculturalists, living in villages, growing crops, and developing a sedentary culture of walls, material goods, education, and literacy. On the other hand were nomadic pastoralists, trained herders and warriors, illiterate and possessing only the few material goods that could practically be carried in their nomadic lifestyles.

Despite their dependence on herding, these nomadic pastoralists had a strong desire for the goods and products produced by agricultural communities. Since they could not produce these goods themselves, they sought to acquire them through trade with their southern neighbors or by force, raiding and pillaging villages.

As a result of this aggression, these literate farming communities wrote about their northern neighbors in less than flattering terms. According to historian Julia Lovell, written historical records reveal early prejudices against the nomadic peoples of the north. "Chinese sources

CHINESE MYTHOLOGICAL HISTORY

While China's written and archaeological record begins with the Shang Dynasty, China's history extends back a quarter of a million years through myth and legend. Ancient tales, passed down through oral tradition, explain some of China's most important cultural values and connections to the earth, sky, and sea. These tales include the story of the three sovereigns: Fu Hsi, Niu Wa, and Shen Nung. Fu Hsi, with a man's head and a snake's body, taught man to fish and invented marriage. Niu Wa was a queen who rebuilt the fallen sky and rescued Earth from a great flood. Shen Nung, with a human body and an ox's head, taught man to farm. These myths help explain China's long history as both a hydraulic and agricultural civilization.

are full of hostile descriptions of rapacious barbarian nomads from the north," Lovell writes. She quotes some of the more colorful descriptions of the nomads as "birds and beasts," as "wolves to whom no indulgence should be given," and as "inhuman specimens covetous for gain, human-faced but animal hearted."[5] In addition to writing about their northern neighbors, the Chinese responded to the clash of values and to their fear of their northern neighbors by building walls—long, strong, and well fortified.

The First Walls

From what archaeologists can tell, walls have long been a part of Chinese culture. The first walls in China probably surrounded homesites. As people settled into communities, however, they began to build longer and larger walls. As communities came into conflict over land use, and as agricultural villages found the need to protect their assets, communities built walls. City walls became a chief feature of Chinese communities. Archaeologists have found evidence of city walls from as long ago as 5000 BC in Zhengzhou, Henan Province. In the six-thousand-year-old village site at Banpo in Shaanxi Province, for example, archaeologists have uncovered evidence of a wall—a moat 20 feet (6 m) across and 23 feet (7 m) deep, surrounding the village site. Walls and moats are thought to have been built as city defenses.

By 2500 BC city walls were a common feature of agricultural communities. By 1500 BC walls protected most agricultural villages from both aggressive neighbors and from pillaging pastoralists looking for goods. Most walls built during this early period used a rammed-earth method in which village laborers packed dirt inside frames and compacted it with mallets. When the frames were removed, a wall remained. As villages joined together into larger city-states over the centuries, larger and longer defensive walls arose, along with a more powerful, class-based social system.

The Divisive Shang Dynasty

Up until 1600 BC much of what historians know about Chinese history comes from the murkiness of myth or from piecing together the archaeological record by examining artifacts. Starting with the Shang Dynasty, in power from about 1600 to 1050 BC, however, written records begin to correspond with archaeological finds. Cities mentioned in written records corresponded with ruins discovered by scientists.

Skilled workers created bronze dagger-axes (pictured) during the Shang and Zhou Dynasties. Written records and archaeological evidence from both dynasties suggest the formation of fiefdoms governed and protected by an established hierarchy.

The Shang arose in Hebei Province, near what is now Beijing, and moved their capital many times over the centuries. They had systems for writing, currency, and calendars, and they were skilled in bronze work and chariot warfare. They also had a sharply defined social system. The Shang were a warlike people with a strong social hierarchy called feudalism.

At the top of society was a ruler who used force, bronze chariots, and weaponry to attack neighboring kingdoms and gain land and slaves. At the bottom of society, just above slaves captured in war, were serfs—landless peasants who were bound to work the land and give the proceeds to the king. In between these two groups were noblemen who were given land by the king in return for a pledge to fight for him and collect tribute from the peasants.

The feudal system and the growing population on agricultural lands made large-scale building projects easier. It also made war an ongoing threat. Peasants in forced servitude could be called up to work on public projects, such as building walls, or to go to war as soldiers. As the population of city-states grew, the population of available soldiers and laborers grew too. Wall-building projects expanded, and wars and clashes increased.

The Shang rulers demanded tribute from many of those with whom they came in contact, including tribes from the north. According to Lovell, "The Shang were constantly at war with the frontier, non-Chinese people they called the Qiang, hunting, capturing and disposing of them as human sacrifices (up to 500 at a time) and slaves."[6] A sharp divide had developed between the cultures of the north and the Chinese of the south.

Wall Building During the Zhou Dynasty

At the end of the Shang Dynasty, the Zhou Dynasty, which ruled from about 1050 to 256 BC, heralded the start of a period of wall building that divided not only the north from the south but also one city from the next. Zhou Dynasty rulers divided the kingdom into more than eight hundred fiefdoms, small areas that were each governed by a nobleman. The noblemen were nominally loyal to the Zhou leaders; in reality, however, the Zhou were in charge in name only. Fiefdoms warred so endlessly among themselves that the period has come to be known as the Warring States period.

As each small fiefdom fought against its neighbors for land and power, they began to consolidate into larger city-states. Some joined together by choice, but others were connected by force into larger and stronger states. Walls became a means of protecting these larger states from each other. Leaders fortified and expanded city walls to encompass far more than a single city, with fortresses, garrisons for soldiers, and beacon towers. Between the fifth and third centuries BC, the state of Qi built the first long wall, a 300-mile (483-km) barrier that included beacon towers, castles, and ramparts. Soon other states did the same.

Long walls were meant to be barriers against other greedy states, but they were also useful against invasions from northern pastoralists. Sometimes states would work together to build walls against a common enemy. In 658 BC, for example, three states joined together to build a wall for protection against raiders from the north. The age of the wall had begun.

CHAPTER TWO

The Unification of China and the First Great Wall

By the end of the warring states period, from a maximum of eight hundred states, fifteen powerful players had emerged from the fray. Among them were the states of Wei, Qi, Qu, Han, Sung, Zhou, and Qin. Of the fifteen, four states were from the north, with different customs and traditions from those of the south. By 325 BC eleven fiefdoms had survived, each claiming its own kingdom with an independent king.

Most of these new kingdoms were greatly influenced by Confucianism, a system in which tradition governed each person's role in the community—from peasant to ruler—and determined each person's behavior through a system of rigid customs and social rituals. Strong traditions meant that everyone knew what to expect from everyone else, from the individual person to the state as a whole.

The Mixed Traditions of Qin

Qin, however, followed different traditions. Located in the northeast, Qin was situated in a buffer zone between the Chinese states and the northern barbarians. Its culture mixed traditions of the north with those of the south. For this reason, the feudal states of the south and east looked down on Qin.

In 266 BC a Wei nobleman wrote to his king to express his concerns about Qin values and practices. The Qin people, he said, knew nothing of the arts favored by the Confucian states; its people did not even play civilized music but merely banged on drums. He wrote, "Qin has the same customs as the Rong and Di barbarians. It has the heart of a tiger or wolf. It is avaricious, perverse, greedy for profit and . . . knows nothing about etiquette, proper relationships and virtuous conduct."[7]

Worst of all, Qin specialized in brazen military might, which was a decidedly un-Confucian endeavor. The structure of Qin's army was especially alarming. It resembled that of the nomads of the north. While Qin leaders claimed descent from the mythical emperors of central China, Qin cavalry resembled that of the northern tribes the Qin had conquered. Qin horsemen were fast and mobile, and they were frightening to states armed with slower-moving chariots and foot soldiers.

The Qin army was supremely disciplined and consisted of three armies working as one. An army of male soldiers worked on battles and defense. An army of women handled provisions and construction of defenses. And an army of old people and invalids looked after livestock and collected food. The three-part army was so effective that it overcame the forces of some of the most important leaders of the time.

In 256 BC the king of Zhou, popularly considered to be "the Son of Heaven," was overthrown by Qin armies. This meant that his mystical objects, the Nine Tripods of Yu (symbols of imperial power), were also in Qin hands—if they could be found. Legends claimed that the tripods had been created by mythical Emperor Yu, tamer of floods. Ownership of the tripods meant possession of power over the element of water. If nothing else, conquering Zhou may have given Qin a measure of psychological supremacy over other kingdoms and lessened resistance to Qin. Sima Qian, a Han historian, later recounted that Qin armies killed 756,000 foreign soldiers and civilians between

275 and 247 BC, with up to 1.4 million dying in Qin wars between 364 and 234 BC. Qin was a force to be reckoned with.

Qin Leaders

While opinions abounded throughout China about the barbarian roots of the Qin, Qin leaders rooted their own ancestry firmly in ancient myth. They claimed the founder of the kingdom was descended from the granddaughter of a distant relative of the fabled Yellow Emperor, and his birth was rumored to be the result of his mother having swallowed a blackbird's egg. The reality was more mundane and politically charged. The first leader was most likely a minor chieftain from the north, an expert in horsemanship, who was granted a small fiefdom in 897 BC and who grew in strength.

The ancestry of Zheng, the man who was to become the king of the Qin in the third century BC, and later the first emperor of China, Qin Shihuangdi, was also the subject of rumor and myth, even in his lifetime. Zheng was the officially recognized great-grandson of the king, son of a prince, Zu Chu, who had been sent to another kingdom as a hostage. While abroad, Zu Chu had fallen in love with a beautiful courtesan. She eventually had a son, Zheng—though some people claimed he was really the illegitimate son of a merchant, a rumor that would later plague the emperor-to-be. Zu Chu returned to Qin, rose to power, and became king. After his untimely death a few years later, his son, Zheng, aged thirteen, rose in line to lead the Qin Dynasty. His most powerful advisers were followers of a tradition called legalism, which had been growing in influence in Qin for the last century. Legalism would transform Qin and all of China.

Legalism

Sometime in the fourth century BC, a philosopher and bureaucrat arrived in Qin with a new way of looking at things. Shang Yang, who had recently escaped from a neighboring state, brought a new philosophy that would transform Qin and, eventually, the rest of China: legalism.

⬡ CONFUCIUS ON WAR AND WALLS

Confucius was perhaps the most influential Chinese scholar in history. Living between 551 and 479 BC, Confucius roamed the countryside offering his wisdom to all. He believed that China had earlier experienced a golden age in which it had achieved power and wisdom through harmony, and that this society could be re-created by adherence to the ideas he set forth.

Confucius and his followers believed that harmony in the home, in the states, and in the world depended on a strict moral code and social hierarchy. Wars and walls were deplorable, Confucian scholars argued, because they disrupted the natural harmony of the world. "When persons and things are in their proper places," dictated by tradition, Confucius said, "relations are smooth, operations are effortless, and the good is sought and done voluntarily."

Confucius advocated for adherence to a strict moral code and a strong hierarchy of power. People, Confucius said, are good but misguided. They need strong, moral rulers to guide them. And rulers must lead because it is their nature and duty to do so. Those on the bottom of the social ladder must take their cues from those on the top. Every person should know his or her place in society.

Quoted in *Internet Encyclopedia of Philosophy*, "Confucius (551–479 BCE)." www.iep.utm.edu.

Shang Yang's legalism was revolutionary. Unlike Confucius and his follower Mencius—both of whom believed that humans are basically good but misguided—Shang Yang, author of some of legalism's most important documents, started with the belief that humans are basically evil. To manage and control this evil nature, therefore, it was necessary to create a clear, authoritative system of laws that would be administered by an absolute and powerful ruler. Unlike Confucianism, which gave each person at birth an unshakable place in a society bound by tradition, legalism taught that society should be governed by laws, behavior controlled through

姓嬴名政始目始皇乙卯即王位庚辰併天下稱皇帝
在位三十七年居王位二十五年即帝位十二年壽五十

China's first emperor, Qin Shihuangdi, created a strong bureaucracy, a uniform legal system, and a powerful military. He believed that a successful society required authoritative laws and an absolute ruler to enforce them.

punishment, and leaders chosen by merit rather than by birth. To a legalist, merit meant military achievement.

Shang Yang was as much a proponent of legalism as he was an opponent of Confucianism. He taught Qin leaders that the traditions advocated by Confucianism were harmful to a healthy state. Drop the traditions, he implied, and power will be yours. If a state follows Confucianism's ten main tenets, he wrote, including "ritualistic conduct, music, poetry, history, virtuous behaviour, morality, filial piety, brotherly obligations, integrity and sophistry, then the ruler will be unable to get his people to fight and the state will fall to pieces."[8]

Shang Reorganizes Qin Society

Qin's legalist state was built around a farming economy. It also had a strong bureaucracy, powerful military, and a legal system characterized by uniformity. It rejected feudalism wholeheartedly. Shang Yang dismantled the last stand of feudal privilege—land ownership—and registered every household to make tax collection more efficient and equitable.

Shang rearranged society into groups of five to ten families who were legally obliged to help each other in farming and other endeavors. Each group was no longer obligated to pay tribute to a feudal lord. Now they were to pay taxes to the emperor. This way of organizing communities made it easier to collect taxes, conscript soldiers, and recruit or coerce labor. The groups were also legally required to reveal crimes committed within the group. Failure to report a crime could result in such punishments as being chopped in two at the waist or being pulled apart by horses or chariots. Ultimately, each group's loyalty was to the supreme ruler rather than to a feudal lord. And no one—not even Qin leaders— was above the law.

Qin law was brutal but effective. Punishments for keeping silent in the face of crime were as severe as those for criminals. Few people in Qin dared to protest the repressive laws. Many were too afraid. Others, however, appreciated the relative security the Qin regime provided compared with the conflicts in the rest of the region.

In addition, the Qin idea of meritocracy—advancement by merit—drew talented workers to Qin from other states in China.

These newcomers hoped to advance through their own efforts rather than be held back by the rigidity of Confucian social order. Additionally, Qin leaders sought to weaken the power of wealthy aristocrats and strengthen the power of average people. "Encourage the poor with incentives so they become richer," Shang wrote, and "penalize the rich so they become poorer. If a state administration manages to make the poor rich and the rich poor then the country will be very strong and will end up on top."[9]

Qin Expansion and Chinese Unification

Legalism's bureaucratic system of high taxation and forced labor made the state wealthy. With its new wealth, the Qin built an enormous and well-organized army with an active cavalry. With it, the Qin swept through China, crushing opposition and annexing surrounding states one by one. As Sima Qian later wrote, "As a silkworm devours a mulberry leaf, so Qin swallowed up the kingdoms of the Empire."[10]

Led by General Meng Tian, the Qin rolled over Zhao, Han, and Wei by 225 BC and then went on to conquer Chu in 223 BC, Yen in 222 BC, and, finally, in 221 BC, Qi. China was now a single, unified empire under a single leader: Qin Shihuangdi, the first emperor of China. With each state that he annexed, the emperor swept away the last vestiges of feudalism in China. He collected weapons and melted them down, ordered guards to kill members of royal families, and forced remaining ruling-class elites to move to the Qin capital under his watchful eye.

In an effort to destroy even the memories of feudal traditions, Qin collected books and burned them—particularly books about Confucianism. The only books saved were those detailing the history of Qin, those on technical topics such as agriculture, and those scholars managed to hide away at the time.

Qin built a large, well-organized army—immortalized in the terra-cotta warrior statues in his tomb (pictured). With his army he was able to crush the opposition and conquer surrounding states.

Unifying and Standardizing an Empire

In expanding his kingdom, the emperor created a centralized government run under the doctrine of legalism. First, he destroyed the long walls between the kingdoms. An inscription from 215 BC memorializes the power of his destruction:

> He has demolished the inner and outer walls of cities.
> He has cut through the embankments of rivers.
> He has leveled the bulwarks and mountain defiles.[11]

MYTHS OF THE QIN GREAT WALL

The building of the first Great Wall has been enshrined in history, poetry, myth, and songs for thousands of years. In one myth, a dragon that has grown tired of flying over China drops to the ground. There, the spines on its back form the wall. Some stories speak of the brutal nature of the work of wall building and the possibility of retribution. The story of Meng Chiang-nu is perhaps the most famous story, memorialized in poetry, song, opera, and even film.

According to the story, Meng Chiang-nu is a beautiful and talented girl who marries a brilliant young scholar. Not long after marrying, Meng's husband is conscripted to work on the emperor's wall as a punishment for his political views. Before long, the hard labor, lack of food, icy climate of the north, and punishments weaken the young man. He dies while working, and his body is buried in the wall.

When Meng goes in search of her husband, she learns that he has died. While hunting for his bones, she accidentally causes part of the wall to collapse, spilling out the bones of thousands of workers just as the emperor, Qin Shihuangdi, is passing by. The emperor sees Meng, instantly falls in love with her, and commands her to join his royal court. She assents, with the condition that her husband be given a dignified burial by the sea. During the burial ceremony Meng throws herself into the sea in hopes of forever joining her spirit with that of her husband.

Once these walls were torn down, Qin Shihuangdi divided the empire into administrative districts, most of which were run by bureaucrats from Qin, loyal and responsible to the emperor himself.

New roads—built to a standardized plan by conscripted peasants—connected all the regions, both for military and trade purposes. Qin Shihuangdi decreed that all roads had to accommodate a standard-sized axle, making military control and movement easier throughout the empire. Road building was only one aspect of the emperor's regime of standardization.

With borders opened and trade expanding, he ordered the standardization of currency and measurements so that each region could more easily trade with one another. Written language, too, was standardized, making it easier for people from one region to communicate with those from another, regardless of differences in dialect.

As trade increased, a strong merchant class rose to replace the aristocracy. While the end of feudalism and aristocratic land ownership might have spelled success for peasants at this time, not a lot changed for the lowest classes. Land taken away from aristocrats passed inevitably to merchants, and former peasants remained as tenants, farming land they did not own to pay land-owning merchants. Peasants, who once would have been forced to work for low-level aristocrats on local wall building, were now considered subjects of the emperor and were forced to work on larger-scale civic projects much farther away: projects such as canals, roads, monuments, and, most importantly, the first Great Wall.

WORDS IN CONTEXT

aristocracy
People holding special privileges, usually due to birth or wealth, who often rule over those without privilege.

Building the Great Wall

Now that the first emperor had unified China, he turned his attention to the problem of the northern barbarians and how to protect his growing empire from attacks.

The emperor, ever paranoid about losing power, had heard a prophecy that one day the tribe of Hu would overthrow him. At the time, Hu was a small tribe in Manchuria in the northeast, and Qin Shihuangdi was more worried about other northern groups, particularly the Xiongnu. The Xiongnu were livestock herders in Inner Mongolia. While General Meng Tian's army had pushed them out of the Ordos region, they were a constant threat, pressing up to the boundaries of Chinese territory. The emperor wanted them stopped, and a long wall seemed like a good way to do this.

Although walls were no longer needed to separate administrative districts, walls were needed to join them together against a common foe. Several former kingdoms—Yan, Zhao, and part of Qin—had long ago created walls to the north as protection against marauding nomads. Qin Shihuangdi ordered that these walls be used as a framework for an even longer wall. He put Meng Tian, his great general, in charge of the project.

The wall project was of an unprecedented scale. It was the first of many *wanli*, or ten-thousand-*li*, walls in Chinese history. It carried a sense of magnificence and hugeness. Qin Shihuangdi was building a really big wall. Han historian Sima Qian, writing from the distance of the next dynasty, describes the wall's origin.

> After Qin had unified the world, Meng Tian was sent to command a host of three hundred thousand to drive out the Jung [Rong] and Ti [Di] along the north. He took from them the territory to the south of the [Yellow] river, and built a Great Wall, constructing its defiles [a narrow gorge through which troops could pass only one at a time] and passes in accordance with the configurations of the terrain. It began at Lintao, crossed the Yellow River, and extended to Liaodong . . . a distance of more than 10,000 *li*.[12]

For the most part, the project simply joined together disparate pieces of already existing walls to create one of unified length and strength. The sections of the wall built during Qin Shihuangdi's reign between 221 and 210 BC combined an estimated 1,300 miles (2,092 km) of previously built walls with at least 500 miles (805 km) of new construction.

To do this work, Meng Tian now had at his disposal hundreds of thousands, if not millions, of peasants from all over the new empire who could be commanded to work on behalf of the emperor. In addition, some thirty thousand families were uprooted from their homes and resettled by force in areas along the wall, particularly in the Ordos region, to provide food and other necessities to workers and soldiers laboring on the wall.

Working on the First Great Wall

The process of conscripting peasants ensured that villagers would provide service. Conscription officers traveled from village to village, recruiting and conscripting laborers for civic projects such as walls, canals, roads, and monuments. The legalist government's requirement that everyone register for taxation made it easy for agents to find laborers. Peasants dreaded the arrival of these agents, for it meant being forced into harsh manual labor for months or even years at a time, far from home. As one poet of the time wrote, referring to the laws written on tablets,

> The king's service brings many hardships,
> We have no time to rest or bide.
> We do indeed long to return;
> But we fear the writings on the tablets.[13]

Peasants who stayed behind and did not work on the wall also dreaded the arrival of government agents because the removal of key family members meant a village could not adequately farm the land, make a living, and pay the taxes imposed by the Qin regime. Conscription broke up communities, stole valuable labor from the countryside, and sent families into debt. As one writer of the period wrote:

> At the present time, out of each peasant family of five persons, at least two are taken away by official press-gangs for

state works. A family is incapable of farming more than 100 mou [about the size of five football fields]. In spring, the peasants work the land, in summer they hoe, in autumn they harvest, in winter they gather in. They go off to cut wood, they serve the authorities, they work in press-gangs. . . . They do not have a single day of rest throughout the four seasons. If they are fatigued by all this they still have to suffer calamities of floods or drought, as well as the cruel requirements of an exacting government, taxes out of season, orders in the morning and counter-orders in the evening. Therefore those who have possessions have to sell them at half their real value, and those without have to borrow money under agreements whereby they will have to repay twice the amount plus interest. That is why there are people who abandon their fields and who sell their children or grandchildren to pay their debts.[14]

The Hazards of Working on the First Great Wall

Working on Qin Shihuangdi's Great Wall was not only costly but also extremely hazardous. The exhausting work of wall building involved moving tons of dirt and stone, pounding loess with iron clubs, and surviving on little food. Conscripted peasants often did not return home—ever.

Qin Shihuangdi often consulted oracles and soothsayers in making decisions of state. One told him that the bodies of ten thousand laborers would need to be buried in the wall for the project to be a

Poor nutrition and brutal conditions, including harsh treatment by overseers, resulted in the deaths of thousands of workers building Qin Shihuangdi's wall. Wall building fell mostly to peasants and convicts who were forced into service.

success. Stories suggest that, instead, the emperor found a man whose name included the word *wan*, meaning "ten thousand," and it was he who was buried in the wall.

Regardless of myth and rumor, however, it is known that thousands of workers died in the building process as a result of the brutal working conditions and poor nutrition.

Many wall builders were convicts. Convict orders were written on bamboo slips, and those that remain from the period describe convicts with shaved, tattooed heads, in scarlet clothes and headscarves, with shackles around their necks and legs, condemned to a lifetime of wall building.

Supervisors on the wall project were often cruel. Every twenty convicts had a supervisor who administered lashes with a bamboo stick for "laziness," with worse punishments for damage to tools or supplies. Food was restricted, too. Convicts who did more work got more food, while those who were sick or doing lighter labor were given less. And convicts who were married had to get food from their own families, regardless of the families' ability to feed them.

While large numbers of convicts and peasants forced into labor died during their efforts, those with some wealth were able to remove themselves from service. Those with money could atone for their crimes by paying fines, and peasants with access to funds could buy off their service or hire someone else to take their place. Labor—and death—along the wall fell to those who were poor and without resources.

Revolt in the Countryside

While Qin Shihuangdi may have hoped the Great Wall would protect his empire's northern border, the brutality of the wall-building process led in part to the end of his dynasty. The first emperor died while embarking upon a journey to the east to find the elusive elixir of life. When he was succeeded by his son, a weak young man placed on the throne by unscrupulous advisers, the countryside erupted in revolt. Convicts forced to work on the wall were the first to rebel.

One rebellion followed another until soon the whole empire was in turmoil. In the ensuing chaos, the aristocracy arose once again in an attempt to regain power. Leaders from the aristocracy succeeded kings who had risen from the peasantry until a prolonged civil war pitted the forces of feudalism against the powers of meritocracy. In the end, the conflict was won by a former village headman, Liu Pang, who rose to become the leader of a new regime—the Han Dynasty—around 206 BC.

WORDS IN CONTEXT

dynasty
Rulers in a line of succession from the same family or lineage.

CHAPTER THREE

China's Relationships with the Tribes of the North

During the Han Dynasty, which lasted from about 206 BC to AD 220, leaders tried everything they could think of to manage relationships with the people of the north. The Great Wall was one of many strategies they used to protect villages, expand the empire, and maintain their way of life.

Liu Pang, the first leader of the Han Dynasty, rose to power at the end of a period of warfare and chaos. Qin Shihuangdi and his successor in the Qin Dynasty were widely seen as greedy and less concerned with the welfare of the empire than with their own personal wealth. Taxation had been a matter of personal gain rather than public benefit. With the empire in financial and civil chaos, Liu Pang began the painful process of reorganizing society and restoring the country's financial health.

His first goal was to wrest power from the merchant class, whom he saw as a symptom of the empire's moral illness—a greedy drain on his kingdom's coffers. He removed them from power through new laws that forbade them from enjoying the trappings of wealth, such as wearing silk. Next, he reorganized the government, dividing the empire into administrative zones, each run by one of his trusted friends or relations.

New Threats from the North

With this process under way, Liu Pang could turn his attention to another pressing problem: managing the northern border. Without money from taxes to run a military operation, wall construction and security had fallen by the wayside. Liu Pang was worried—and with good cause.

In the northern states along the border, there were signs that the barbarian nomadic tribes were gaining power and becoming better organized. One tribal group in particular, the Xiongnu, was gathering power under a leader named Tu-man. Tu-man had taken advantage of the chaos and power vacuum in China and had moved his people deep into the Ordos, as far as the Yellow River. When Tu-man was overthrown and killed by his own son, the brutal Mo-tun, a power vacuum appeared in the north. Seeing the change in leadership, other nomadic tribes tried to gain power from the Xiongnu by stealing horses, women, and land. Mo-tun and the Xiongnu responded decisively by brutally sweeping through the tribes of the north like a storm, taking land and animals and consolidating power.

WORDS IN CONTEXT

nomad
A person with no fixed home who travels around.

Rumors of Mo-tun's brutality quickly spread throughout the Chinese empire. Mo-tun, it was said, had not only killed a rival chieftain but had made a drinking cup of his skull and lined it with silver to serve as a warning to those who might challenge his power. Mo-tun was a man to be reckoned with.

In his palace, Liu Pang and his advisers heard these stories about Mo-tun. They heard rumors that Mo-tun and his soldiers had taken control of parts of the Great Wall. The humiliation of having the very tribe the wall was designed to keep out now in control of it irked Liu Pang. The wall had the potential to stop great battalions of cavalry. But if the barbarians controlled even one gate in the wall, all was lost. In the empire's impoverished state, paying for a regular garrison of

The royal entourage of Liu Pang, the Han Dynasty's first leader, makes its way over a mountain pass. Liu rose to power during a period of chaos and war.

soldiers to live at the wall was now too expensive. Liu Pang and his advisers began to rethink how to manage the tribes of the north. If the wall could not contain the nomads, how could they be controlled?

Military Campaigns in the North

Mo-tun acted before Liu Pang and his advisers had time to decide what to do. Mo-tun and his men surrounded Ma Yi, a city in Chinese territory. Liu Pang's relative, stationed there and in charge of the city government, surrendered. Mo-tun and his men continued their march south. Military engagement looked inevitable.

In bitter cold, Liu Pang led his army against the invaders. Mo-tun retreated, his men following as he fled back to the north. Liu Pang and his army, suffering frostbite and other challenges from the cold, followed. The retreat, however, turned out to be a trap. Mo-tun had concealed a much larger army out of sight. When Liu Pang and his men reached the city of Ping Cheng and stopped to rest, Mo-tun surrounded the city with four hundred thousand horsemen. The two sides remained in a stalemate until Liu Pang managed to smuggle out an adviser, who contacted Mo-tun's wife in the hopes that she could persuade the nomad to give up the fight. In time, however, both sides realized that a true and decisive victory would be impossible. Neither one could successfully rule the other's territory, so the leaders and their armies returned home.

Liu Pang was not the last emperor to try to conquer the Xiongnu militarily. As the Xiongnu continued to plague the border regions, many military campaigns ventured north. Over time, Chinese generals began using the tactics of the Xiongnu themselves. They learned how to breed horses and ride and fight from horseback. Some of the most successful generals, in fact, were of mixed descent or came from the steppes themselves and had grown up with these cavalry skills. Fighting horsemen with horsemen was better than pitting foot soldiers against cavalry. But while military engagement held the Xiongnu back and even damaged their long-term ability to attack the Chinese, nothing stopped them for long, and the border problems continued. Other tactics were needed to contain the Xiongnu.

Engaging the Enemy

Some emperors tried to woo the Xiongnu with goodwill. They wondered whether attacks could be averted with gifts of Chinese products. After the failure of his military campaign, Liu Pang showered Mo-tun and the Xiongnu with presents. Silk thread and cloth, bronze, and grains passed through the border to the Xiongnu leader. Treaties and tributes, or gifts, were recorded in official registries. And when Mo-tun's men raided the border occasionally, the emperor's subordinates issued only a mild reproach.

Another tactic the Chinese used to try to engage and appease the Xiongnu was marriage. Intermarriage had long been a tactic

⬡ IRON AND SALT

After the fall of the Qin Dynasty—widely seen as greedy and excessive—Han leaders had to stabilize the economy. At that time the government had not been in charge of minting coins. Anyone who found copper on his property could make coins. This created inflation—prices that rose out of control. Prices of other commodities also rose when merchants gained monopolies on an industry. Around 81 BC Song Hung-yang, an adviser to the emperor, suggested that the government take control of some aspects of the economy in order to break merchant monopolies and stabilize prices. To prevent inflation, he advised the government to take charge of minting coins and controlling the price of two essential commodities: salt and iron.

State ownership, or nationalization, of industry resulted in a great debate among government officials that was recorded by Han-era historian Sima Qian. The debate centered around the idea that making a profit led to the loss of a moral society, and if the government made a profit, then the government would be immoral.

> If a country possesses a wealth of fertile land and yet its people are underfed, the reason is that merchants and workers have prospered while agriculture has been neglected. . . . A spring cannot fill a leaking cup. . . . This is why [Han Dynasty founder Liu Pang] . . . prohibited merchants and shopkeepers from becoming officials. Their purpose was to discourage habits of greed and to strengthen the spirit of sincerity. . . . How much worse it would be if the ruler himself were to pursue a profit!

Quoted in Patricia Buckley Ebrey, ed., *Chinese Civilization: A Sourcebook*. New York: Free Press, 1993, pp. 60–63.

used worldwide by royal families to cement bonds between nations, and the Chinese were no different. Liu Pang sent a Chinese princess, a girl of royal blood, to marry Mo-tun. She was the first of many princesses sent by Han emperors to the Xiongnu. The intention was to form a blood tie between the two nations so that the Xiongnu would no longer attack those who were now their relatives. Although the tactic may have been popular among the Xiongnu, the Chinese public was horrified by this action. Offering their royal girls to the Xiongnu was repulsive to them. Nonetheless, the marriages continued, as they appeared to keep war at bay—at least temporarily. One legend tells of an emperor named Yuan who, in 48 BC, dreams of a girl whom he then sends across the border to marry the Xiongnu chieftain, Khujanga. She accepts the ways of the northern peoples, and the union brings peace and stability to the region.

The Wall as a Gateway

Nothing worked for long to contain the Xiongnu, however. Every Han emperor had to find a way to manage the border. Some looked beyond the idea of the wall as a barrier and began to see the wall as a place to export the high, settled, and literate culture of the Han to an expanding world. The adoption of Han culture and values would make the northern peoples feel more connected to the empire, the reasoning went, and thus less likely to attack it.

Emperor Wen Ti, who ruled from about 180 to 157 BC, hoped to expand the empire and bring non-Chinese people under his control in precisely this way. To this end, Wen Ti sent an envoy to the north to learn more about the Xiongnu people. On his return, the envoy reported that the Xiongnu had different tastes and different needs than the Chinese. "If only they acquired the taste for our things, and had only one-fifth of our needs, they would become our tributaries,"[15] wrote the envoy in his report to the emperor. Later emperors would expand on this idea, seeking to increase trade with the Xiongnu and create a friendly market for Chinese goods and ideas.

Colonization was another way some emperors sought to export Chinese culture, goods, and ideas to the north. In 120 BC Emperor Wu, who ruled between about 140 and 87 BC, ordered one hundred

Chinese leaders adopted some of the fighting tactics of their northern neighbors, including the use of cavalry and chariots. Cavalry and chariots carved in bronze illustrate military innovations of the Han Dynasty.

thousand Chinese peasants to resettle in the Ordos region. Laborers created new extensions of the Great Wall, created irrigation canals, tilled the soil, and planted crops. The new agricultural area was intended to provide a buffer zone and perhaps an area of exchange between the cultures of the north and the south. But Emperor Wu did not reckon on the region's climate. There was a reason only nomads lived in the area: it was not well suited to agriculture. When the Yellow River flooded, killing thousands of the new settlers, the project was all but abandoned.

Diplomacy

Emperor Wu also tried the path of diplomacy and alliance building to control the Xiongnu. He sent an envoy, Chang-Qian, to talk to the Yueh-chih, a northern tribe that had previously been conquered by the Xiongnu. His plan was to convince the Yueh-chih to go back to their homeland and force the Xiongnu to leave it. The discussion was delayed when Chang-Qian was captured by the Xiongnu and held for ten years. When he at last escaped, he made his way to the Yueh-chih and met with their leaders. Unfortunately, they rejected his plan. They had no interest in trying to regain lost lands.

On his way back to Emperor Wu, Chang-Qian was captured once again and held for a year. When he was finally released, Chang-Qian returned to the emperor with no good news—but instead with a rich variety of products, plants, and animals from the west, including a species of horse that appeared to sweat blood. Today scientists believe that the horses were probably infected with a skin parasite that caused them to appear to sweat blood. Whatever the cause, the emperor was fascinated, and a few years later he sent Chang-Qian on a series of missions to establish trade and acquire horses. By the end of the Han Dynasty, the Great Wall was no longer a barrier but a guide pointing to the trade routes with the west.

Soldiers at Work

During the Han period, security at the Great Wall consisted primarily of small units of conscripted soldiers manning watchtowers and signal towers and keeping an eye toward the north on the Xiongnu. To catch intruders, soldiers kept watch in shifts day and night. They also spread fine sand at the base of the wall so that the footprints of intruders could be seen in the morning.

As in past dynasties, many soldiers labored at wall building. During this period they built towers made mainly of brick, plaster, and whitewash. The tops of the towers consisted of a platform with crenellated walls stocked with cocked crossbows that were ready to fire. The towers also held armor and helmets; grease and glue for repairing equipment; clay pots for storing water; braziers, pots, and dried dung to build fires and cook food; and a medicine chest. In addition, some towers also contained poles for raising signal flags and torches for giving signals at night.

WORDS IN CONTEXT
commodities
Goods and services.

Some soldiers were not assigned to military duties at all but rather were stationed in agricultural villages nearby to help grow food for those living and working at the border. Agriculture was no easy task, as water was scarce and the land hard and infertile. Complex irrigation systems and walls were built to protect crops from the whipping winds and frequent dust storms. Protection systems were also built to prevent the Xiongnu from sabotaging irrigation systems or harming those who were working on these public works projects.

Life along the wall during the Han Dynasty, even for soldiers, was not all bad. While soldiers were still conscripted from warmer and more hospitable areas of the south and were fewer in number, they were better equipped and better fed than previous generations of soldiers. And although the northern border could be cold and lonely, volunteer soldiers often brought their families with them. Officers living along the border could own their own homes, horses, slaves, and land.

Many of these details of Han life are known today because the Han Dynasty was a time of excellent record keeping. All grain harvested and brought to storage centers near the wall was measured and recorded, as was the distribution of grain to frontier colonies. From archaeological exploration that has yielded detailed records of trade, food, weaponry, and building methods, historians have been able to construct a complete picture of life during the Han Dynasty—including the building and maintenance of the Han wall.

Trade Along the Wall

Trade along the wall, both agricultural and commercial, was monitored and recorded by soldiers stationed at the frontier. The wall ran east and west along the expanding trade routes that would become what was later known as the Silk Road. Goods such as silk and ceramics were carried west to the expanding Roman Empire. Western products, such as furs, rugs, and jewels, were carried back. Ideas traveled along the Great Wall, too. Music, science, and inventions such as gunpowder made the transit from China to Europe and back along the wall's Silk Road.

Soldiers on the wall bore the great burden of monitoring movements. Soldiers checked travelers who wanted to cross the wall into China. They checked lists of "undesirables" (such as criminals), searched through travelers' luggage to prevent smuggling, and checked official documents of people waiting to cross the barrier. Soldiers at the border maintained good records of who went through the wall, and some of these records remain today as historical documents.

Trade introduced Chinese society to new ideas and provided unprecedented opportunities for building wealth. An official, reporting on the state of the empire after Emperor Wu's death, wrote:

A piece of ordinary Chinese silk can be traded with the Xiongnu for articles worth several pieces of gold, and thus we are able to whittle down the resources of the enemy. Unbroken chains of mules, donkeys and camels cross the frontier. The Imperial Treasury is filled with the furs of sables, marmots, foxes and badgers, patterned rugs and carpets, while jade, charmed stones, corals and crystals are added to the national wealth. The people enjoy abundance.[16]

◆ OFFICIAL DOCUMENTS ON MANAGING THE XIONGNU

The Han Dynasty, expanding its empire into central Asia for purposes of trade, often ran into trouble with Xiongnu nomads. A government minister during the reign of Han Wendi (202–157 BC) argued in favor of colonizing the frontier north of the Great Wall in order to drive back the Xiongnu. The government minister stated:

The Xiongnu eat meat and cheese, wear skins and fur, and possess no farmstead or field. Want of grass and water keeps them migrating. They lurk along the border, ready to invade. It would profit the emperor to dispatch generals, officials and troops to colonize the frontier. Families should be resettled there to farm fields. High walls and deep ditches should be built to hinder the Xiongnu's southerly advances.

Quoted in William Lindesay, *Images of Asia: The Great Wall*. Oxford: Oxford University Press, 2003, p. 22.

The influence and power of the Han Dynasty rose and fell over the centuries. By about AD 190, however, the Han reign had ended, and China was once again divided—this time into three parts: Wu and Shu in the south, and Wei to the north. China entered a long dark age in which north and south were ruled separately, and China once again became socially stratified, with a powerful aristocracy at the top, and peasants, laborers, and slaves at the bottom. A series of non-Chinese dynasties came to power, mixing elements of Chinese and northern cultures.

The Mixing of Cultures

After the fall of the Han Dynasty, the northern kingdom of Wei was ruled by leaders who had roots in the far north. These northern rulers had a dilemma. In ruling large swaths of the region, they were venturing into the territories and cultures of agriculturalists. Their northern nomadic herding way of life could not succeed on land divided into many small farms. The only way to rule successfully was to settle down.

WORDS IN CONTEXT

pastoralism
A social system based on dependence on herding domesticated animals.

As these once-tough northern nomadic tribes began to settle down, however, they began to lose their nomadic ways and, some said, become soft. According to historian Julia Lovell, these tribes faced a dilemma: "whether to remain tough nomadic warriors or submit pleasurably to the civilized creature comforts of the settled Chinese culture."[17] Nomadic pastoralists began to take on the ways of the agriculturalists. A mixing of civilizations was occurring that would radically change the cultures on both sides of the wall.

The pastoralist Wei leaders from the north found they could not govern Chinese villages in the same way they had ruled tribal nomads on the steppes. Agriculturalists were literate and settled. They were used to well-ordered lives that included taxation and art, walls, and farming. In order to rule these farmers, the Wei had to give up some

Spear-wielding soldiers resembling these terra-cotta statues from the Han era manned watchtowers along the wall. They kept watch in day and night shifts, vigilant against possible intruders.

of their traditional ways of living, including the primary defensive use of cavalry. But giving up the cavalry left them open to attack from other northern tribes. In response, the Wei took a decidedly Chinese approach to the problem: they built walls.

Ultimately, the walls built by northern tribes proved to be less about defense and more about show. Ruling a land with a mixed ecology—part steppe and part farmland—was not easy. It required the new dynasties to think in two ways. On the one hand, they learned to govern their new lands in a Chinese way: as an organized bureaucracy. On the other hand, with other nomadic tribes on the attack, they had to be able to outthink and outsmart the nomads militarily.

Cultures mixed in other ways, too. Some northern tribes hired themselves out as a sort of "cavalry for hire" to Chinese emperors. This gave them a way to make a living while protecting Chinese assets. But this period did not last long. By the year 304 many of these hired swords were ready to fight for themselves and found their own states.

The Tang Dynasty

The Tang Dynasty grew from the mixing of Chinese and northern aristocratic families. In peacetime, the Tang Dynasty ruled through bureaucracies that collected taxes. When times were less peaceful, however, they used swift and brutal punishments that brought to mind the bloody ways of the tribes of the steppes.

Early on, Tang cities were cosmopolitan places, full of immigrants from all over Asia, the Arabian Peninsula, and even Europe. These foreigners brought new arts and crafts, new cultural traditions, and new attitudes toward women. These foreigners helped turn Chinese cultural conventions upside down. The idea that China was at the center of civilization, for example, stood on shaky ground in the face of such a strong foreign influence. Chinese walls—not only a physical barrier but also a mental barrier between all that was Chinese and everything that was non-Chinese—were neglected in favor of military tactics and diplomacy.

Neglect of the Great Wall left China open to attacks from the north and from within. In the eighth century, new leaders arose who rejected the Tang values of diversity. They tried to curb attacks on the wall by issuing a series of xenophobic proclamations intended to strengthen Chinese society. Between 700 and 850, the Tang Dynasty began issuing complaints about foreigners, forbidding the Chinese to have contact with non-Chinese. They also issued a proclamation seizing the land and property of Buddhist monasteries for use as public buildings.

In the succeeding centuries China was ruled by a succession of clans from the steppes of the north. Each found it a struggle to balance the culture of the north—pastoralist, nomadic—with the culture of the south—literate, agricultural, and settled. Despite these difficulties, the region was now a veritable blend of cultures.

CHAPTER FOUR

The Mongol Threat and the Ming Dynasty

etween AD 900 and 1100, a blend of cultures lived along the border region between China and the north. In the early 900s the Khitan people unified parts of Inner Mongolia and southern Manchuria and gained control over the Great Wall. Their leader, Apaochi, used battalions of skillful, mounted archers to attack neighboring tribes and bring them under control. With an army of twelve battalions—seventy thousand men—the Khitan were unstoppable. The only thing they could not do, as Apaochi was well aware, was govern the nations they conquered. For that, Apaochi believed he needed Chinese bureaucrats and agriculturalists.

Over the next few centuries the Khitan pressed southward, fighting their way into China and creating a society that had both farming and herding elements. Never one to give up land or power, the Chinese Sung Dynasty pushed back. Finally, in the early part of the new millennium, the Khitan and Sung armies realized that neither could defeat the other. They chartered a peace agreement, agreed to respect each other's boundaries, and agreed not to add any additional walls or canals in the border region.

While peace between the Khitan and Sung lasted for about a century, other nomadic groups were on the move, battling for control of small parts of the region. During this period the Great Wall had a new purpose—protecting northern nomads from cultural incursion by the Chinese. Around 1100, the Nuchen, nomadic warriors, gained control of northern China. To protect their cultural identity, the Nuchen enacted many laws to prevent Nuchen citizens from taking on Chinese customs, names, and traditions. They also extended the wall some 500 miles (805 km) into the north and built many smaller sections of wall as protection against other tribes. They did not know how much these would be needed in a few short years.

The Rise of Genghis Khan

While the Khitan and Nuchen were battling for power in the lands of the north, the Mongols were living relatively peaceful lives as nomadic herders. Some clans were hunters and fishermen in the far north. Most, however, were nomadic herders who moved with their flocks with each season. Life on the Mongolian plains was harsh. The Mongols ate a carnivorous diet, supplementing meat with the milk of their flocks and blood drawn from the opened veins of their still-living horses. They lived in tents, called yurts, created from skins and felt made from the wool of their flocks. They lived by the rule of "survival of the fittest," with men eating first, women next, and children last. Children learned at an early age to be independent and resourceful.

WORDS IN CONTEXT
battalion
An army unit of one or more groups of soldiers.

In the year 1167 a baby named Temujin was born to the head of a Mongol clan. According to legend, at birth Temujin emerged clutching a clot of blood—a sign, the soothsayers said, of greatness to come. Although his father died when Temujin was still young, like all Mongol boys, Temujin learned the skills of a hunter and warrior. He learned to ride hard on his horse, shoot an arrow with

Genghis Khan and his soldiers overrun and capture a Chinese town, as depicted in this sixteenth-century artwork. No walls could keep the charismatic but brutal Mongol leader out of China.

astonishing accuracy, and fight fearlessly for access to the pasture-lands of the steppes. When he was thirteen, he became a khan, or leader of his clan.

Temujin began his career by leading attacks against rival clans, moving through the Gobi swiftly and decisively, soon bringing the entire region under his control. In 1206 he called for a *kurultai*, a council of khans from across the steppes. The time had come, he said, to choose a leader for the region, an emperor. It was no surprise that Temujin was elected leader and was named Genghis Khan, "Emperor of All Men."

Genghis Khan's First Foreign Conquests

By all accounts, Genghis Khan was a charismatic leader who demon-strated both fairness and great brutality. He gave his people a code of law, some of which was directed at demanding loyalty to himself. The law also commanded the people to follow a strict moral code. Those who violated the laws faced stiff penalties. For theft, lying, spying, black magic, and adultery, violators faced death.

WORDS IN CONTEXT

bureaucrat
An official rigidly attached to administrative details.

Genghis Khan seems to have had his mind on conquest from the start. Some ac-counts claim that he told men that there was no greater joy in life than to "conquer one's enemies, to pursue them, to deprive them of their possessions, to reduce their families to tears"[18] and steal their horses and wives. After bringing the steppes under his control, Genghis Khan set his sights on the south, to the lands beyond the Great Wall.

In 1209, with an army amassed from the collective strength of all the Mongol clans, Genghis Khan began his first campaign against a

"foreign" tribe. The Tangut, who lived at the western end of the Great Wall, had little chance of survival against the onslaught of such skilled warriors. Other tribes did not fare much better. Many gave up without a fight, choosing to ally with the Mongols rather than face their wrath. With such easy victories under his belt, Genghis Khan turned to larger quarry—the Nuchen Empire.

In 1211 a massive Mongol army gathered at the border of the Nuchen Empire. The Nuchen, who up until this time had paid little attention to the Mongols, were not worried. They had a new emperor on the throne and had asked the Mongols to pay tribute. Genghis Khan, naturally, refused. Instead, he is said to have replied that his army would come upon the Nuchen like a roaring ocean, whether they were met by friends or foes. The Nuchen, he said, could rule their own lands under the leadership of Genghis Khan if they chose. If they chose to resist, the Mongols would attack and fight to the finish.

The Mongols marched south into Nuchen territory, heading for the Nuchen capital, Yenching. Genghis Khan was not worried that the Great Wall stood in his way. In fact, he and his army pushed through the smaller outer walls and chose a route that would run into the strongest and most heavily fortified part of the Great Wall. When they reached the gate at Chu Yung Kuan, however, they stopped. There, a 40-foot-high (12 m) wall surrounded the capital and was heavily fortified with moats, watchtowers, stone forts, and arsenals containing a new invention—gunpowder-propelled rockets. When his attack on the capital failed, Genghis Khan led his men west to a less-fortified area, where before returning home they slaughtered the Nuchen guards and the local tribe who guarded that part of the wall.

Mongol Demands

In 1214 Genghis Khan led his army on a second campaign across northern China. Divided into three battalions, they attacked three different areas, with Yenching reserved for Genghis Khan himself.

⬡ THE TIGER SEALS AND TABLETS

Seals and tablets were used to identify soldiers and deliver messages. Seals and tablets were engraved with identifying information and carried from place to place, in much the same way that identity cards are carried today.

When orders were given by a military commander in the capital and conveyed to soldiers in the field, the officer bearing the message carried half of a tally (*bing fu*) or seal (*yin*). The seals of commanders bore the symbol of a tiger. One half of the seal went into the field with the soldiers, and one half stayed with the commander. When the messenger arrived to deliver the message, carrying the half seal, the two halves would be put together, proving that the orders were indeed from the commanding officer. When the mission was completed, the two halves of the seal were returned, ready for the next use.

Rectangular tablets were also used to identify which soldiers or officers were authorized to be in a particular place at a particular time. Soldiers patrolling the Great Wall, for example, tied different types of tablets to their waists while they were on duty. Inscribed on the tablets were instructions such as, "Defense troops must wear this tablet. Failure to wear it is punishable by law."

Cheng Dalin, *The Great Wall of China*. Hong Kong: South China Morning Post, 1984, pp. 218–19.

Using the techniques of swift attack and siege, and wearing leather armor and spiked metal helmets, they moved through the countryside, capturing towns and driving away frightened farmers. Yenching, however, once again proved too difficult a prize. Seeing that his men needed to regroup and regain their strength before winter set in, Genghis Khan decided to return home. Before the army left, however, he demanded a prize from the emperor: a princess for himself, one thousand slaves, a herd of horses, masses of gold, and quantities of silk cloth.

In his eagerness to have them leave, the emperor agreed to the Mongol's demands. As soon as the intruders were gone, however, the emperor left for his southern capital, leaving his unfortunate son in charge of Yenching to face an angry and rebellious public. The Mongols did not go far. They stopped at the Great Wall, and Genghis Khan waited while a delegation of five thousand soldiers went back to Yenching and took the city.

Genghis Khan was more of a conqueror than an administrator. Despite the fact that he had broadened his empire, he was not particularly interested in running it. Rather than administer his new provinces himself, he chose to leave the administration of his lands to others and continue his progress across Asia and into Europe. Between 1214 and 1227, Genghis Khan fought bloody battles over lands to the west. When he died in 1227, his third son, Ögödei, took up the mantle and expanded the empire.

Kublai Khan Takes Control of China

Under the leadership of Ögödei Khan, and Genghis Khan's grandson, Kublai Khan, the Mongol Empire expanded across Asia and into Europe. In 1231, the Mongol armies took Korea; in 1235, Moscow, and by 1251, Persia, Mesopotamia, and Syria. By the time Kublai Khan came to power after 1259, the Mongols were already working their way south into China.

Despite the weakness of the Sung rulers of southern China, the Mongol armies had difficulty controlling the region. For one thing, the Mongol method of warfare—sweeping in on horses with arrows flying—did not work in a swampy region of rice paddies. For another, the population was much denser in the south. That meant there were many more people to fight back. The Chinese of the south were not the pushovers the Nuchen had been. Some cities fought off sieges for years. By 1280, nonetheless, most of China was under Mongol control.

As leader of both the Chinese and the Mongols, Kublai Khan adopted a Chinese dynastic name, Yuan, and was known both as the great Mongol khan and the emperor of China. In Chinese lore he continued to be just another incompetent barbarian. To the Mongols, however, he was a brave leader of a magnificent people.

During the Yuan Dynasty, the Mongols living in China continued their own cultural traditions. They created a caste system that put the Mongols on top; other non-Chinese, such as Persians, in a second-class citizen status; Nuchen citizens in third place; and Sung Chinese on the bottom of the social ladder. This discrimination would be one of many seeds that would incite Chinese rebellion. The Mongols also taxed the Chinese heavily, though they used some of these taxes to make improvements in China. They expanded the country's transportation system, building roads and canals with a labor force of 2.5 million men, and initiated a complex mail system with couriers and two hundred thousand horses.

By the mid-1300s, however, the Mongol Empire in China was in decline. Rebellions arose throughout China against the Mongol Yuan Dynasty. Rival leaders battled for turf. Finally, a leader, Shu Yuanshang, rose up from Anhwei province and gained control over much of southern China. With an army of 250,000 men, he marched north to what is now Beijing and drove the Yuan emperor and the Mongols out of China. Shu Yuanshang became emperor of China and established the Ming Dynasty—considered by some to be the greatest wall builders China has ever known.

The Ming Wall

Shu Yuanshang was eager to keep the recently expelled Mongols out of China forever. He put his sons in charge of different sections of the Great Wall and gave them the task of protecting China from attack. At first they responded to Mongol threats with offensive attacks against the nomads north of the wall. These thrusts into enemy territory were effective for a time, and the Mongols were driven back repeatedly. But ultimately, using an offensive strategy was an expensive and unsustainable method of protecting the border. In the Ordos region, for example, control of the land transferred back and forth from Chinese to Mongols for centuries. By the late 1400s the Mongols had swarmed back in, bringing their herds and pressing south. A stronger, more permanent solution was needed to keep the Mongols out.

In 1399 leadership of China fell onto the shoulders of Chu Ti, who came to be known by the title of Yung-lo, or "Perpetual Happiness." Chu Ti defeated the Mongol leader of the time, Alutai, and forced him to declare allegiance to the Ming Dynasty. Chu Ti also moved the Chinese capital from Nanking to what is now Beijing—a location much closer to the Great Wall. From this new vantage point, Chu Ti could better control the frontier.

In his new capital, Chu Ti became obsessed with strengthening the wall. He took note of the size and shape of the sections that had effectively kept out the Mongols in the past, and he tried to re-create them in new areas of the wall. He redesigned sections of the wall to be higher, stronger, and more functional. The wall surrounding the old Nuchen capital, for example, had withstood a Mongol invasion for months. Chu Ti used the wall's design to make the Great Wall better. He instructed builders to create a wall that was 40 feet high (12 m) and 15 feet wide (5 m). It was to be made with a core of alternating bricks and limestone, with huge stones on the outside and bricks many layers thick. The result was a wall that in many places was like a fortress, wide enough and strong enough on top to support a host of soldiers, with many crenellated edges for firing weapons through.

Work on the Great Wall accelerated in the late 1400s. It followed the natural terrain, twisting and turning back on itself just as rivers swirled and looped, scaling precipitous ridges, or crossing plains in a maze of ditches and walls two or even three layers deep. Ultimately, Ming additions to the wall increased its length by 5,499 miles (8,850 km).

Building a Better Wall

Building, lengthening, and strengthening a structure this large required a massive human resources effort. For much of the Ming Dynasty, the army was almost solely responsible for construction, main-

Thousands of laborers ensure that work on the Great Wall moves steadily forward. The Ming Dynasty is considered by some historians to be the greatest of China's wall builders.

tenance, and guarding the Great Wall. Some 860,000 soldiers were stationed there over a fifty-year period. Some sections were built by permanently stationed garrison soldiers, but in other places and times visiting garrisons of soldiers would construct a specific project, such as a gateway.

Building the Ming wall was a brutally difficult process. Work was divided up so that small sections of the wall were the responsibility of small groups of builders. Builders began by digging two parallel trenches that they lined with flat stone slabs. Using these stones as a base, they began to build two walls, using the limestone and other materials that were available to them in that particular location.

THE MING MILITARY ORGANIZATION

The Ming military, which at times boasted a force of roughly 860,000 soldiers, operated within a complex hierarchy. At the top was the *Bing Bu*, or Military Department, similar to a Ministry of Defense. It was commanded by three governors appointed by the emperor, each of whom was in charge of a separate region. Each region was divided into nine garrison zones, or *zhen*. Each *zhen* was responsible for a segment of the Great Wall, on both the inside and outside. Each *zhen* was divided into a *wei* of 5,600 men and again subdivided into *quanhu suo*, which meant one thousand households of 1,200 men. Each of these was, in turn, subdivided into groups of 120, 50, and 10.

Status in the military was often conferred by heredity. Many of those in the armed forces were part of a permanent, hereditary military classification called *jun ji*. Those with *jun ji* status were obliged by birth to enter the military upon reaching adulthood. *Jun ji* soldiers were often permanently stationed in a garrison along with their families.

Other soldiers formed part of a shifting army of recruits. These soldiers, many of whom were conscripted during wartime, worked at whatever tasks were needed. These tasks ranged from wall building to warfare.

Although they used local materials, stone boulders and slabs still had to be transported to the spot where the wall was being built—not an easy task in the days before mechanization. While a few animals may have been used to carry stone, mainly it was people—poor laborers—who became the beasts of burden. Many workers died from overwork and poor nutrition during the process.

When the wall reached a few feet high, workers filled it with rubble, rocks, earth, and limestone. Workers then climbed on top and pounded the rubble down with long poles and mallets to make it hard and solid—the same rammed-earth process used by earlier Chinese. When the rubble inside reached the height of the outer framework, it was topped off with stones, and that section of the wall was complete.

The terrain of the Great Wall made building difficult. In many places the wall followed a harsh terrain of ridges and peaks. Workers carried stone pieces up steep terrain using baskets. With this painstaking labor, the Great Wall rose, tall and strong.

The suffering surrounding the building of the Ming wall inspired a wealth of ballads, poetry, and folklore. Ming-era balladeer Yin Geng sang, "Nothing was pleasing in the wall construction in the last year. The blood of the builders flowed by like a moat."[19] Ming poet Li Mengyang wrote, "An order has been issued this year for the construction of the wall. One half of the drafted laborers have been worked to death at its foot."[20]

Convicts were also sent to work on the wall as punishment for any of 213 different offenses. For example, a person who wounded another with a sharp weapon could be sent to the wall as part of a work gang. And government officials convicted of corruption or forgery could be banished to the wall to serve their sentences. Convicts served two types of sentences for hard labor on the wall: lifetime and perpetual. While being sentenced to a lifetime of slave labor on the Great Wall of China might sound bad, a perpetual sentence was worse. It meant that not only did the convict have to work on the wall until death, but the convict's son, grandson, great-grandson, and so on also had to serve. For capital offenses, a convict could save his life through perpetual service. If a man had no son, another relative could serve the punishment. If there were no relatives, a neighbor would have to serve in place of the criminal.

Work Along the Wall

Not everyone working along the Great Wall was involved in its construction. Farmers were recruited to grow crops to feed the garrisons of soldiers. These military farms produced thousands of tons of grain per year, and they often grew into towns that included soldiers' wives and families.

Emperor Zhu Yuanzhang also ensured that soldiers working on the wall had enough food by manipulating another sector of the

Chinese economy—the salt trade. While the Ming Dynasty, like the Han before it, claimed a monopoly on salt production, it awarded contracts for selling and distributing salt to merchants in exchange for grain. Merchants who delivered large quantities of grain to the Great Wall received larger quantities of salt to sell. Because transporting grain to the Great Wall was expensive, merchants who owned land and created farms along the wall had an advantage over those who did not. As a result, merchants scrambled to set up farms along the wall. The emperor is said to have boasted, "I have been able to support a million soldiers there without using any of the grain of the civilians."[21]

Soldiers fulfilled a variety of jobs along the wall. With a border thousands of miles long, the Ming needed a way to convey messages—particularly about attacks—over long distances. Signalers sent messages between sections of the wall. At watchtowers, soldiers manned signal stations to send messages between towers. During the day flags and smoke were used to send messages. Smoke signals, once made with wolf dung, were now made by adding sulfur and saltpeter to special burners on each tower. Different chemicals produced different colors of smoke—red, black, purple, and white—to send different messages. Different colored flags also conveyed different messages. For example, one yellow flag meant an enemy force was approaching with fewer than one hundred soldiers. A sheepskin meant a force of five hundred to a thousand men were coming.

At night lanterns, bonfires, and even cannon fire provided the means of communication. Different numbers of lanterns conveyed different messages. Four lanterns, for example, meant that an enemy force of five thousand to ten thousand was approaching, and cannon fire meant that the enemy was attacking. If an attack continued, the signal was repeated every two hours.

The Last Great Wall

The Ming Dynasty continued building and rebuilding the Great Wall until the dynasty's final days. The Ming wall reached China's eastern coast. There, just beyond Shanhaiguan, the fortress known as the First Great Pass Under Heaven, the wall enters Bohai Bay in the Yellow Sea. The gigantic structure, built of three-ton blocks of granite, was intended to thwart intruders by forcing them into the sea. Instead, Shanhaiguan was ultimately one of the wall's weakest points. It is at this site in 1644 that a Ming general allowed Manchu battalions to pass through the gates and enter China to fight off rebels. This event marked the beginning of Manchu dominance of China, the establishment of the Qing Dynasty, and the end of Ming rule.

At its height, the Ming wall system included nearly 5,500 miles (8,851 km) of new wall, with some sections two, three, or even four layers thick. For hundreds of years the wall played a vital role in protecting China. After the Ming Dynasty, however, the wall played a much less prominent role in China's defense. For one thing, the decline of the Mongol Empire meant fewer threats from the north. Although Mongol leaders made brief attempts to regain power, such as the uprising of Mongol khan Galdan, they were ultimately crushed by Chinese strength.

The Great Wall also lost its relevance for another reason: intermarriage. As Chinese and Mongols intermarried, Mongol culture was changed and diluted. The Qing

Dynasty, originally Manchus of the north, was a blend of northern and southern cultures. To the Manchus, the wall was porous—more of a monument than a barrier.

Chinese migration also made the Great Wall irrelevant. By the 1700s Chinese settlers had moved into Mongolian territory in masses. The wall became a landmark of a different era, and Inner Mongolia became a part of China. Over time the Great Wall crumbled, its bricks and stones used by villagers for the needs of everyday life.

CHAPTER FIVE

The Great Wall in Modern Times

Today the Great Wall is a study in contrasts. In some places it is a revered and well-preserved symbol of Chinese culture and ingenuity while in other places it is a crumbling relic of bygone days. Some early European visitors to the wall during the Manchu Dynasty, which ruled China from 1644 to 1912, noted its magnificence. One such visitor, Ludovic Hebert, the Marquis de Beauvoir, wrote, "It is a supremely wonderful sight! To think that these walls, built in apparently inaccessible places, as though to balance the Milky Way in the sky, a walled way over the mountain tops, are the work of men, makes it seem like a dream."[22]

Others commented on the growing evidence of its decline, describing it as a crumbling and unappreciated historical artifact. John Thomson, the author of a four-volume folio of travel pictures in 1873, wrote that he found the Great Wall "neither picturesque nor striking," and that it was "the greatest monument of misdirected human labour to be met with in the whole world." He added that "its masonry is often defective."[23]

While serving some small defensive purpose during the Sino-Japanese War (1937–1945), the wall did not take on its present significance as a symbol of Chinese greatness until after 1949. From that time onward, the Great Wall has served as one of China's primary symbols of human endeavor, ingenuity, and greatness.

Preserving the Great Wall

In the early 1960s the Chinese government, for the first time in modern history, recognized the wall as an important cultural site. Twenty-five years later the world recognized its importance as well. The United Nations (UN) Educational, Scientific, and Cultural Organization listed the Great Wall as a World Heritage Site in 1987. As a World Heritage Site, the wall became part of a network of more than nine hundred natural and cultural icons around the world. The UN World Heritage Committee chooses sites it believes have a value to humanity's understanding of the earth, human culture, and history. Gaining this status gave the Chinese government impetus and funding for preservation and the ability to attract history-minded preservationists from around the world.

Throughout China and throughout the world, nonprofit grassroots organizations have raised money and interest in preserving the wall. The China Great Wall Society, founded in 1987, notes on its website that it is devoted to the "study and publicizing of the Great Wall to promote its exploration and protection. Its task is to foster traditional Chinese cultures, carry forward the Great Wall spirit, bring into full play its functions as a bridge between the government and society, and mobilize all social forces available to protect the Great Wall."[24]

As part of its mission, the China Great Wall Society created the Great Wall Museum at Badaling, near Beijing and close to some of the most monumental of the Ming sections of the wall. The group not only works to raise money to preserve the wall and develop the museum but also creates an understanding of the history of the wall through education efforts, and it campaigns to educate and encourage those who live near the wall to preserve and protect it. To this end, the society creates and distributes films about local customs and ethnicities along the Great Wall. It also supports theatrical, orchestral, and art performances and exhibitions about the wall.

One of the group's most important projects involved mapping the entire length of the Great Wall for the first time. Using space satellites equipped with advanced remote sensing technology, the China Great Wall Society worked with the Chinese government to discover, document, and map the extent of China's long walls. In June 2012 the Chinese State Administration of Cultural Heritage published the results of the geographic survey. According to that survey, the Great Wall is approximately 13,170 miles (21,195 km) long. Of that length, 5,499 miles (8,850 km) were built during the Ming Dynasty, and 7,671 miles (12,345 km) were built in previous periods. CNN reported that these measurements include not only existing walls but also places where only remnants of the wall remain. "Among the 5,499 miles [8,850 km] in the Ming Dynasty section . . . 223 miles [359 km] were trenches and 1,387 miles [2,232 km] were natural defensive barriers such as rivers or steep hills that were incorporated into the wall system."[25]

In addition to measuring the wall, the China Great Wall Society and the government have worked together to organize a "ten-thousand *li*" inspection of the wall. The study revealed that the wall is crumbling. "In some sections, only the foundation remains; and only 8.2% of the walls from the Ming Dynasty are whole,"[26] according to the Xinhua News Agency.

Gathering information on the state of the Great Wall has been essential to its preservation. From this information, the government now has data and tools with which to formulate a new Great Wall protection law. The China Great Wall Society has been both a champion and a voice for the wall, hoping their efforts will ensure the wall's integrity far into the future.

Threats to the Wall

Despite the society's preservation efforts, China's government has had difficulty balancing the wall's historic importance with contemporary needs. Tourism and construction projects, mining, reconstruction, and even preparations for the 2008 Olympics have threatened the well-being of the Great Wall. Public works projects such as road building have destroyed or threatened sections of the

The Great Wall snakes through a mountainous section of China. A recent survey that relied on satellites equipped with remote sensing technology found that the wall is more than 13,000 miles (20,800 km) long.

wall in recent years. In 2003 a construction company working on roads to connect country lanes to a freeway knocked thirty 131-foot (40 m) holes in Ming Dynasty walls to make way for the road. Electricity projects, communications cables, natural gas lines, watering systems, and mining and forestry projects have also put the integrity of the wall at risk.

Developers, often with government approval, have tried many different schemes to attract tourists to the wall. Many of these efforts, undertaken in the name of restoration, threaten the wall's historical integrity, notes a 2007 *National Geographic* article. "Poorly executed restoration efforts have left sections near the capital, Beijing, looking like a Hollywood set. Entrepreneurs have set up cable cars, souvenir stalls, fast-food restaurants, amusement facilities, villas, and crowded parking lots—all within a stone's throw of the structure."[27]

GREAT WALL KITSCH

Trade in wall-related items near many areas of the Great Wall provides many Chinese with a way to make a living outside of the officially sanctioned tourist trade. Trinket and souvenir stands sell everything from tiny terra cotta warriors and miniature Great Walls to Chinese nesting dolls, pandas, teapots, chopsticks, and busts of Chairman Mao. Green plastic carvings marketed as jade, icons of the Chinese zodiac, necklaces, and fans all promise buyers good luck and a prosperous future. And all, of course, bear a familiar label: *Made in China*.

Generally, the greatest damage has come from those living close to the wall. One reason for this is a lack of education about the wall's historical significance. *National Geographic* reports some recent incidents of damage to the wall: "Three men in Inner Mongolia were detained for taking earth from an ancient 2,200-year-old section of the wall to use as a landfill for a village factory. 'It's just a pile of earth,' village head Hao Zengjun told the official Xinhua News Agency."[28] Another reason people living along the wall cause damage to the ancient structure is economic. China's booming economy has meant that the entrepreneurial spirit driving economic growth has reached the Great Wall. Locals sometimes work hard to turn their particular section of the wall into the largest tourist attraction possible—often through unregulated activities.

Some people living near the ancient structure have damaged the wall while using it as an unofficial tourist destination. *National Geographic* reports that in some areas, farmers have cemented over centuries-old sections of the Ming wall and created gates so they can charge admission. In what is perhaps a misguided attempt to repair nature's own reclamation of the wall, in some places tourists have taken a turn at weed pulling, removing grass from rammed-earth walls until they crumble to dust. In another area, locals have nailed Christmas lights to towers dating back to the fourteenth century.

In 2002 the World Monuments Fund, a nonprofit organization based in New York, placed the Great Wall on a list of the world's most endangered historical sites. Historian William Lindesay says it was a "wake up call" for the Chinese government. The next year, new government regulations came into play, calling for greater protection of the wall. "The government has clearly made the protection of the Great Wall a national effort,"[29] Lindesay says. It is now illegal to carve on the wall, remove bricks or stones from it, hold large parties on the wall, and build structures against it. The new laws also assign all Chinese citizens, organizations, and entities with the job of protecting the wall and reporting to authorities any damage. "The law states

Tourists swarm a popular section of the Great Wall near Beijing in 2012. Modern pressures, including tourism, traffic, and construction threaten to undermine sections of the ancient wall.

what can and can't be done, and it says who's responsible. And it defines society's responsibility to protect the Great Wall,"[30] says Dong Yaohui, the chairman of the China Great Wall Society

The Wall as a Political Icon

Preservation efforts have been essential to keeping the Great Wall physically intact. Not all threats to the wall have been physical, however. Throughout the 1800s the wall was derided and ignored as a relic of the past. Its importance as a symbol of China's rich history and cultural heritage was resurrected by Sun Yat-sen, the first president and founder of the Republic of China in 1912. Sun served as leader of the Chinese Nationalist Party until 1949, and he is considered one of the most important political leaders of modern China. He described the Great Wall as one of China's greatest engineering feats, which allowed the nation to develop strength while living in peace. His words began to change the Chinese view of the wall from ancient relic to cultural icon.

Massive shifts in China's political culture during the 1940s threatened to undo this new attitude toward the wall. A civil war between Chinese Nationalist forces and Chinese Communists ended with the victory of Communist forces in 1949. Communist leaders were reluctant to connect their revolution with the wall's despotic builders, particularly China's first despot, Qin Shihuangdi. Rather than abandon this gigantic icon of China's past, however, they embraced the Great Wall as a symbol of Chinese greatness, persistence, and ingenuity. During the Long March (October 1934–October 1935) in which Chinese Communists fled the Nationalist forces, Communist leader Mao Zedong wrote a poem:

WORDS IN CONTEXT

communism

A system in which all property is held in common by the community.

> We've scored a march of twenty-thousand li.
> We shall the Great Wall reach,
> Or no true soldiers be.[31]

This poem represented a new view of the Great Wall among Communist leaders, one that was echoed in song and film. One song redefines the role of the Great Wall in a new China, calling on the nation's people "to take our own flesh and blood, to build a new Great Wall!"[32]

Today the Great Wall is a potent symbol of China's aspirations. Foreign leaders visiting China are routinely taken to the wall. The first such visit was part of US president Richard Nixon's historic trip to Communist China in 1972. He told the press at the time, "This is a Great Wall and it had to be built by a great people."[33]

Quotes about the wall are used as inspiration throughout modern Chinese society. Mao's iconic quote, "You're not a hero if you don't get to the Great Wall,"[34] printed in Mao's own calligraphic handwriting, is paired with photos and paintings of the Great Wall in political advertisements throughout China. The Great Wall, despite its beginnings in forced peasant labor and imperialist ambition, has become a symbol of Chinese Communist ideals of honest hard work and equality.

Commerce and Tourism at the Great Wall

While the Great Wall is a political and cultural icon for the Chinese people, it also represents a commercial opportunity for China's newly developing entrepreneurial spirit. It provides a livelihood for everyone from tour guides to trinket manufacturers and vendors, to architects and builders designing Great Wall replicas, and to actors playing roles of historical figures along the wall.

Ever entrepreneurial, the Chinese people know good branding when they see it, and the Great Wall is among China's best-known symbols, ready to be used by merchants to achieve their new capitalist dreams. The image of the Great Wall appears on everything from Chinese money to advertisements for Great Wall–branded products. For example, billboards and ads in many parts of China promote Great Wall wine, perhaps associating the vintage and power of the wine with the age and gravity of the wall.

The shape of the wall has inspired imitators of a most commercial stripe. In 1983 the first commercial hotel built following the Cultural Revolution of the 1960s and 1970s, in which China destroyed many artistic relics of the past, was built in Beijing near the wall. Built-to-scale crenellated walls attract tourists. In other places in China, other faux Great Walls have sprung up, with requisite tourist infrastructure such as a luxury boutique hotel near Badaling called the Great Wall.

Although much of tourism along the wall is highly regulated by the government, with highly trained and officially sanctioned tour guides to help tourists understand the history of the Great Wall, unregistered guides abound. One such guide explained her reasons for foregoing the official test and registration in an interview recorded by researcher Sang Ye and translated by Geramie R. Barme. In the interview she expresses her sense of ownership of the wall and a certain sense of disregard for official rules:

> I don't think having a license is necessary for a guide. I've got what it takes, even if I haven't done the exam and don't work for a travel agency. To be allowed to take the test you have to undergo training, and that costs money. Not to put too fine a point on it—their business is selling licenses. What does the tourism bureau manage? They manage to take your money! Our ancestors left the great Wall to all of us. I have as much a right to make a buck out of it as they do. More to the point, I'm a worker who lost her job, and I've given myself this one in order to look after my family. What's wrong with that?[35]

Living with the Great Wall

Some in China feel that the wall has become too commercial. Zhang Jun is webmaster of A Small Site on the Great Wall, a website that strives to protect the Great Wall. His project called "I Live with the Wall" encourages visitors to photograph ordinary people who live along the wall today. He hopes these photographs will help reduce commercialization of the wall and encourage its preservation and historical integrity. Some people living along the wall, he says, try to make a living in destructive ways that cause long-term problems for short-term gains. "Many villagers living by the Great Wall, or near to it, dig mines, fire bricks, dig canals, build roads and hunt for scorpions in the cracks on the wall—all activities that threaten to destroy it. The aggressive development of tourism is also very detrimental."[36]

Zhang has been disappointed by commercialization of the Great Wall for another reason: It detracts from the wall's historical significance. "When I first came to Beijing for university I rushed out to see the Great Wall at Badaling, but was bitterly disappointed. It was a noisy bazaar, a theme park." When Zhang saw pictures of an unrestored, unreconstructed section of the wall for the first time, however,

⬡ THE 2008 BEIJING OLYMPICS

In August 2008 China hosted the world's athletes in the XXIX Olympics. The Great Wall figured prominently in Olympic materials, advertising, and tourism as a symbol of China's ancient and modern gifts and strengths. The Chinese government also resurrected the specter of the wall as a defense against danger with its Great Wall 5 antiterrorism drills, developed in preparation for the Olympics. According to China's Xinhua News Agency, the displays of military might involved "police forces, the People's Armed Police, the People's Liberation Army and the health, environmental protection, meteorology and transportation departments." Through drills involving military vehicles, martial arts, and weaponry skills, China's Great Wall 5 showed the world that it was prepared for anything at the Olympics.

Quoted in The Big Picture: News Stories in Photographs, "Anti-Terrorism Exercises in China," July 9, 2008. www.boston.com.

and then visited the site near Simatai, he knew he wanted to work to preserve the integrity of the Great Wall. "I will never forget the grandeur and sense of history conveyed by those images," he says. "So that's what the Great Wall was really like!"[37]

Zhang believes that the Great Wall's deepest value is as a cultural symbol. "It is a crucial link for the study and understanding of the history of our multi-ethnic country," he writes, and should be preserved "to respect both history and the future."[38]

The Great Wall in Modern Art

In addition to its historic significance, the magnificence and grandeur of the Great Wall has made it a stage and backdrop for art of all kinds. Artists from around the world have gravitated toward the wall to showcase their works. In 1979 French fashion designer Pierre Cardin used the wall as a backdrop to premiere his spring/summer clothing collection. In elaborate shows and fashion shoots, willowy European models in gauzy gowns of rainbow colors pranced in the winds on Badaling's restored wall while Chinese workers in drab colors looked on.

From the mid-1980s onward, Chinese artists have felt the freedom to explore the subject of the Great Wall through both ordinary representational paintings and symbol-laden work. Paintings of the Great Wall are often created on a monumental scale. One such painting is often used as the backdrop for official photographs of Chinese diplomats and political figures with heads of state from foreign nations. And at Chinese international airports such as in Beijing, gigantic paintings of the wall remind visitors of the greatness of Chinese civilization.

Artist Xu Bing, expounding on the idea that the wall represents the monumental futility of human efforts in the world, created a work of art of epic proportions. With the aid of fifteen people, thirteen hundred sheets of paper, three hundred bottles of ink, and four months of labor, Xu took rubbings of sections of the wall and pieced them together. Titled *Ghosts Pounding the*

Wall, the artwork was displayed in China and in the United States in 1991 and 2005.

In a more experimental piece, Cai Guo Qiang created *Project for Extraterrestrials No 10: Project to Extend the Great Wall of China by 10,000 Metres*, a 1993 performance art piece that was also preserved through photography for a permanent display. After laying a 32,808-foot-long (10,000 m) line of encased gunpowder from the Great Wall into the Gobi Desert at the westernmost section of the wall, Cai lit a fuse. A line of glowing, golden fire, like the back of a great dragon, zipped across the mountainous desert in a spectacular pyrotechnic display. Since each of the elements involved in the art event—gunpowder, dragons, and the Great Wall—are symbols of Chinese power-

WORDS IN CONTEXT
pyrotechnic
Of or related to fireworks.

er, the artwork represented a powerful moment in Chinese artistic freedom. In his artistic statement, Cai said that his goal for the project was to "recapture the soul of the wall by transmitting signals to the universe."[39]

Chinese folk artists and ethnic minorities also use the wall as a subject for art pieces. The art of cutting paper into images—somewhat like cutting snowflakes from white paper—is said to have been carried from one side of the wall to the other through a diplomatic marriage alliance between a Xiongnu ruler and Wang Zhaojun, a beautiful Han Chinese princess around 33 BC. Today ethnic minorities along the Chinese border with Mongolia use paper cutting as a way to express both cultural pride and to describe day-to-day life.

Cui Qingmei is a paper-cutting artist living in the Inner Mongolia area of China near the Great Wall. In her intricate paper cuttings, Cui often depicts life along the wall—her children herding sheep outside the wall, people passing through the wall for work, and family life, food, and home scenes inside the wall. These paper cuttings have a cultural significance to her, and the art and artistic skills have been passed on throughout the community for generations.

The Great Firewall of China

China's Great Wall has taken more than one form over the years, particularly with the advent of the Internet. In 1987 one man with a slogan, "Go Beyond the Great Wall, March Toward the World,"[40] took an enormous first step in opening up the psychological and political boundaries of China and connecting the nation with the world. The man, a professor of computer science at a Chinese university, sent the first Chinese e-mail. From that time to the present, Chinese Internet use has grown exponentially, from 40,000 users in 1995 to 100 million users in 2005 to more than 512 million users today.

The Chinese government has always maintained a tight grip on the media due to the fear that too much freedom would lead to chaos and revolution. While Chinese society has become increasingly open in recent years, and the Internet is officially recognized as playing an important role in commerce, the Chinese government still looks for ways to maintain a Great Wall—dubbed "the Great Firewall"—around the information reaching the Chinese public. Maintaining that wall is increasingly difficult. In 2000 US president Bill Clinton predicted that the Chinese government would find "controlling the Internet is as slippery as 'trying to nail Jell-O to the wall.'"[41]

Despite comments such as this, the Chinese government has maintained this firewall with software that scans the Internet to see whether anyone in China is using words deemed dangerous or offensive. Anyone typing the words *Falun Gong*, the name of a religious group, into a web browser, for example, would find their computer frozen and unusable. Web search engine Google was blocked from China entirely in 2002 for making information too accessible. In 2004 the nonprofit group Reporters Without Borders estimated that 61 "cyber dissidents"[42]—people researching forbidden information on the Internet—were being held in Chinese jails. Despite the Great Firewall of China, the Internet has played an important role in opening Chinese government

Young Chinese play online games and surf the Internet at a popular Internet café. The government's efforts to control information available over the Internet have been dubbed the "Great Firewall"—a name that plays on the symbolism of the Great Wall of China.

and business to scrutiny from within China. Local corruption and cover-ups have been harder to maintain when the eyes of the public are upon officials and the voices of the public are crying out through the Internet.

China's Identity Is Tied to Its Walls

Over thousands of years, China's walls have become an important part of the Chinese cultural, political, and social identity. Whether these walls are virtual, psychological, or built firmly of stone or pounded loess, the Great Wall of China remains both a barrier and a gate of entry between China and the outside world and a symbol of China's sense of itself as a great and separate nation.

SOURCE NOTES

Introduction: Great Wall, Great People

1. Claire Roberts and Geremie R. Barme, eds., *The Great Wall of China*. Sydney, Australia: Powerhouse, 2006, p. 16.
2. Quoted in Roberts and Barme, eds., *The Great Wall of China*, p. 26.

Chapter One: Before the Great Wall

3. Quoted in Keith Buchanan, Charles P. FitzGerald, and Colin A. Ronan, *China: The Land and the People: The History, the Art, and the Science*. New York: Crown, 1980, p. 55.
4. Jonathan Fryer, *The Great Wall of China*. London: New English Library, 1975, p. 20.
5. Julia Lovell, *The Great Wall: China Against the World, 1000 BC to AD 2000*. New York: Grover, 2006, p. 35.
6. Lovell, *The Great Wall*, p. 37.

Chapter Two: The Unification of China and the First Great Wall

7. Quoted in Lovell, *The Great Wall*, p. 50.
8. Quoted in Fryer, *The Great Wall of China*, p. 35.
9. Quoted in Fryer, *The Great Wall of China*, p. 29.
10. Quoted in Buchanan, FitzGerald, and Ronan, *China*, p. 162.
11. Quoted in Lovell, *The Great Wall*, p. 54.
12. Quoted in Arthur Waldron, *The Great Wall of China: From History to Myth*. Cambridge, UK: Cambridge University Press, 1990, p.17.
13. Quoted in Cheng Dalin, *The Great Wall of China*. Hong Kong: South China Morning Post, 1984, p. 16.
14. Quoted in Fryer, *The Great Wall of China*, pp. 62–63.

Chapter Three: China's Relationships with the Tribes of the North

15. Quoted in Fryer, *The Great Wall of China*, p. 81.
16. Quoted in Fryer, *The Great Wall of China*, p. 87.
17. Lovell, *The Great Wall*, pp. 94–95.

Chapter Four: The Mongol Threat and the Ming Dynasty

18. Quoted in Fryer, *The Great Wall of China*, p. 130.
19. Quoted in Cheng, *The Great Wall of China*, p. 197.
20. Quoted in Cheng, *The Great Wall of China*, p. 197.
21. Quoted in Cheng, *The Great Wall of China*, p. 215.

Chapter Five: The Great Wall in Modern Times

22. Quoted in Waldron, *The Great Wall of China*, p. 209.
23. Quoted in Roberts and Barme, *The Great Wall of China*, pp. 18–19.
24. China Great Wall Society, "Great Wall Society," May 5, 2008, www.greatwallculture.org.
25. CNN, "New Survey's Big Surprise: China's Great Wall Much Longer than Previously Estimated," *This Just In* (blog), June 6, 2012. http://news.blogs.cnn.com.
26. Quoted in CNN, "New Survey's Big Surprise."
27. Paul Mooney, "Great Wall of China Overrun, Damaged, Disneyfied," May 15, 2007. http://nationalgeographic.com.
28. Mooney, "Great Wall of China Overrun, Damaged, Disneyfied."
29. Quoted in Mooney, "Great Wall of China Overrun, Damaged, Disneyfied."
30. Quoted in Mooney, "Great Wall of China Overrun, Damaged, Disneyfied."
31. Quoted in Waldron, *The Great Wall of China*, p. 216.
32. Quoted in Waldron, *The Great Wall of China*, p. 216.
33. Quoted in CNN, "New Survey's Big Surprise."
34. Quoted in Roberts and Barme, eds., *The Great Wall of China*, p. 36.

35. Quoted in Roberts and Barme, eds., *The Great Wall of China*, p. 251.

36. Quoted in Roberts and Barme, eds., *The Great Wall of China*, p. 33.

37. Quoted in Roberts and Barme, eds., *The Great Wall of China*, p. 34.

38. Quoted in Roberts and Barme, eds., *The Great Wall of China*, p. 34.

39. Quoted in Roberts and Barme, eds., *The Great Wall of China*, p. 24.

40. Quoted in Lovell, *The Great Wall*, pp. 339–40.

41. Quoted in Gady Epstein, "China's Internet: A Great Cage," *Economist*, April 5, 2013. www.economist.com.

42. Quoted in Lovell, *The Great Wall*, pp. 339–40.

FACTS ABOUT THE GREAT WALL OF CHINA

Size and Age
- The Great Wall is not one single wall but rather many walls built together.
- The walls were built over twenty-four hundred years, from 475 BC to about AD 1644.
- The Chinese word for "great walls" is *wanli changcheng*, or "ten-thousand-*li*-long walls."
- The Great Wall is currently thought to be 13,170 miles (21,195 km) long and stretches across fifteen provinces, from Shanhaiguan Pass on the East China Sea to the western Jiayuguan Pass in Mongolia's Gobi Desert.
- The wall ranges in height from 10 to 33 feet (3 to 10 m) and from 7 to 16 feet (2 to 5 m) in width.
- Archaeologists have mapped 14,721 sites related to the Great Wall.
- Only 8 percent of the original Great Wall remains standing today.

History
- The Great Wall was built to separate settled farming communities from nomadic herding civilizations.
- The first emperor, Qin Shihuangdi, created the first Great Wall by linking existing walls together.
- The Ming Dynasty undertook the largest wall-building project.
- During the Qin Dynasty (221–206 BC) much of the wall was built during a ten-year period.

Construction
- The wall was built by 300,000 soldiers and more than 3 million laborers, most of whom were forced into servitude.

- Many people died building the wall, but it is unclear whether rumors that people were buried inside the wall are true.
- Walls were made of local materials. Because of this, they blend into the landscape.

Modern Chinese Views

- Among Chinese citizens surveyed on a popular Chinese website called SOHU.com, 34.3 percent of respondents had not been to the Great Wall, and 45 percent believe the wall is in poor repair. Also, 2.2 percent admitted to defacing or vandalizing the wall in some way.
- The Great Wall is mentioned in China's national anthem with the words "to build our new Great Wall with our very flesh and blood."

FOR FURTHER RESEARCH

Books

William Lindesay, *The Great Wall Revisted: From the Jade Gate to Old Dragon's Head*. Cambridge, MA: Harvard University Press, 2008.

Julia Lovell, *The Great Wall: China Against the World, 1000 BC to AD 2000*. New York: Grover, 2006.

John Man, *The Great Wall*. London: Bantam, 2008.

Joseph O'Neill, *The Great Wall of China*. Mankato, MN: Abdo, 2009.

Claire Roberts and Geremie R. Barme, eds., *The Great Wall of China*. London: Lund Humphries, 2007.

Websites

ABC News, "Great Wall of China Longer than Previously Reported" (http://abcnews.go.com/blogs/headlines/2012/07/great-wall -of-china-longer-than-previously-reported). This page includes information about recent efforts to map the Great Wall.

Smithsonian.com, "The Great Wall of China Is Under Siege" (www .smithsonianmag.com/people-places/great-wall.html). This Smithsonian museum site provides general information on the Great Wall and includes information about the state of the wall today and efforts to preserve it.

UNESCO, "World Heritage List: The Great Wall" (whc.unesco .org/en/list/438). This website includes information on the history, preservation, and cultural value of the Great Wall.

World Heritage Sites, "The Great Wall of China" (www.global mountainsummit.org/great-wall-of-china.html). This site offers information about the Great Wall and other World Heritage Sites. It also includes a visual tour of important sites along the wall.

INDEX

Cover: Thinkstock Images

© Burstein Collection/Corbis: 42

© Corbis: 46

© imaginechina/Corbis: 13, 71, 73, 81

© Royal Ontario Museum/Corbis: 21

© Keren Su/Corbis: 31

Thinkstock Images: 6, 7, 17

Steve Zmina: 10

Qin Shi Huangdi First Emperor of Qin Dynasty/Universal History Archive/UIG/The Bridgeman Art Library: 28

Slaves building the Great Wall of China (colour litho), Min, Yang Hsien (20th Century)/National Geographic Image Collection/ The Bridgeman Art Library: 37

Warriors with Spears, Shanxi Region (terracotta), Chinese Western Han Dynasty (206 BC-24 AD)/private collection/De Agostini Picture Library/The Bridgeman Art Library: 51

Genghis Khan captures a Chinese town, miniature from the 'Persian History of Genghis Kahn' completed in 1596, Persian School, (16th century)/private collection/Peter Newark Military Pictures/ The Bridgeman Art Library: 57

Building the Great Wall of China, McBride, Angus (1931-2007)/ private collection/(C) Look and Learn/The Bridgeman Art Library: 63

ABOUT THE AUTHOR

Cindy Jenson-Elliott is the author of ten books of nonfiction for children and hundreds of articles for children and adults. She lives in southern California.